RESTLESS WAVE

Illustrations by Eitaro Ishigaki

RESTLESS WAVE
MY LIFE IN TWO WORLDS

A Memoir

AYAKO ISHIGAKI
(writing as Haru Matsui)

Afterword by Yi-Chun Tricia Lin
and Greg Robinson

THE FEMINIST PRESS
at the City University of New York

Published in 2004 by the Feminist Press at the City University of New York, The Graduate Center, 365 Fifth Avenue, Suite 5406, New York, NY 10016
feministpress.org

Originally published in 1940 by Modern Age Books, New York. This edition published by arrangement with Ishigaki Memorial Hall.

Library of Congress Cataloging-in-Publication Data

Ishigaki, Ayako, 1903–1996
   Restless wave : my life in two worlds, a memoir / by Ayako Tanaka Ishigaki ; afterword by Yi-Chun Tricia Lin and Greg Robinson.— 1st Feminist Press ed.
   p. cm.
Originally published: New York : Modern Age Books, Inc., 1940.
   I. Title.
   AC146.I73233 2004
   305.48'8956073'092—dc2   2003023263

Publication of this book was supported by public funds from the National Endowment for the Arts.

NATIONAL
ENDOWMENT
FOR THE ARTS

Printed on acid-free paper by McNaughton & Gunn in the United States of America.

09 08 07 06 05 04   5 4 3 2 1

Acknowledgments

The author wishes to express her deep appreciation for the invaluable literary assistance of Genevieve Blane Birk.

She also wishes to thank Kimi Gengo, Dorothy Colby, Rose Black, and Rae Heim. The author is grateful to Cokesbury Press for permission to quote from *Songs from the Slums,* Toyohiko Kagawa, 1935.

Contents

PART THREE

PART FOUR

PART ONE

Prologue

OUT OF THE PAST the scene becomes vivid—my first memory. I can still see them, those women straining at the ropes and chanting under a clear autumn sky. Those women who made firm the foundation of our house. The house in which we were to live. The house in which Younger Brother was to be born. The house which would see birth and death and daily struggle. The house which would be spotless and well kept and would hide the deep struggle.

These women remain with me. The sun burned their faces, the heat smeared them with dirt and sweat. Their broad grins bared white teeth.

The busy hum of men sawing and nailing rang

3

clear in the autumn air. The timbers smelled strong of new wood. The freshly dug earth was red. The ropes hung lax from the log of the pile driver. Half a dozen women bent their backs and gripped the ropes. They tugged, and the huge log rose. They relaxed, and the log fell hard, pounding the foundation trench. The ground so leveled would make firm the building's foundation. A single high voice started a chant, and others joined the chorus as the lamenting thud of the huge log kept time with the chant.

The women were clad in dark kimonos, their sleeves tucked up in the back. White leggings sheathed their legs. Over their feet were black, rubber-soled socks. Sweat streamed from their foreheads. Their heads were protected from the sun by printed towels. On the backs of a few of them, babies were strapped securely. Babies bending and lifting with their mothers, with the log, with the chant. Gagging, gurgling, crying, sleeping babies, strapped to their mothers' backs. Hungry babies.

The rest period came. The women dropped to the ground in a circle, wiping the sweat with printed towels. Mothers bared their large breasts and suckled their young. They laughed and joked with the men. In loud voices.

They frightened me, these women. I ran, afraid, to my father. Are these strange people who work with men, banter their men, roll up their sleeves—are they women?

4

These women are no longer strange to me. I have seen them everywhere, working, singing, laughing with their men. These women no longer dismay me. I have seen them again and again bending their backs to support their young. These women no longer make me fear. I can see them occupying the house whose foundation they make firm. These women give me hope.

Early Memories

ELDER SISTER and I were dressed alike, in kimonos of the same pattern, with obi-sashes of the same color. In winter we wore thickly padded kimonos. I buried my neck in my collar like a turtle, and looked like a round ball. We had long black hair, brushed to a lustrous shine, hanging down our backs.

Elder Sister Nobu was a bright, attractive girl. Her black eyes danced with laughter and sparkled with wit. But I was slow in mind and action. Elder Sister teased me, saying, "You can move faster rolling than walking on your feet." I looked upon her with admiration, but sometimes with resentment.

We played tag and skipped rope in the garden facing the living room. When we played tag, I found the pool beyond the garden a great handicap. It was shaped like a bottle-gourd for sake wine, narrow in the middle. At the narrow part lay an islet which served as a stepping stone across the pool. Elder Sister Nobu jumped over the islet to reach the other side. She was light, and as fast as a rabbit. But I was heavy. My feet were too short. I had to run all around the pool to tag her, and by that time she was over the hill on the other side. "How slow you are, Haru!" she called down to me. "Catch me if you can!" She squatted and beckoned, laughingly. I was defeated.

I was shy and wretched when invited to meet guests. My throat parched, and my face turned red. I could only hide behind Elder Sister and depend on her for my answers. No wonder nobody was attracted to me.

My grandmother pitied me. "You are gentle and obedient, Haru," she said. "You will make an ideal bride when you grow up. I shall recommend you as bride to a large family, where you can live with your husband's parents. They will be pleased with an obedient daughter like you."

My grandmother's praise made me happy. I dreamed of myself as a beautiful bride in long-sleeved bridal kimono and glossy hairdress studded with flowered jewels. Throughout my childhood and into my teens I was docile and obedient, holding my grandmother's ideal as my ideal. She took pride in the unselfishness, submissiveness and endurance of a Japanese wife. The Code of Greater Duties of Women, drawn up in the seventeenth century, taught that woman's highest obligation is obedience to man: to her father before marriage; to her husband when

8

she marries; to her son if she becomes a widow. To my grandmother, complete submission was the highest virtue of woman.

I was born in Tokyo, in the last stage of the Meiji period. Japan was no longer the dreamland of Hiroshige's beautiful prints. Smoky cities had sprung up all over the country. Wars had been fought with China and with Russia. Things were changing, breathlessly. Old and new clashed everywhere. Feudal Japan had jumped with a single bound into a new age. But my grandmother refused to see any change. She wished her grandchildren to live in the past customs of her own childhood.

It was not only my grandmother. Even those who considered themselves modern could not cast off inconsistent traditional conceptions. Girls were taught the value of exercise and then made to sit stiffly, legs under them, knees close together, eyes straight ahead, and faces blank. Educational ideas from Western countries were coming into the schools, but they were supposed not to conflict with semi-feudal customs. I lived my childhood in the old tradition.

I never saw my father so happy as the day his son was born. Elder Sister and I had been sent to Grandmother's so as not to disturb Mother while she gave birth. When we returned home, Father rushed out to welcome us, saying, "It is a boy baby!" He embraced Elder Sister, and lifted her high over his head.

Elder Sister screamed with joy, "A baby brother!" She twisted her lips like a grownup. Knowing it

9

would please Father, she said, "Honorable Father, you look very, very happy."

Father burst into a laugh and tickled her under the chin. "My little daughter knows everything, doesn't she?" He became excited like this very seldom.

I, the younger, stood silently, unnoticed by Father, wondering what a baby brother looked like. It was a hot summer day. The new baby, wearing a white silk gown, was sleeping in a high crib screened by mosquito net. A nurse lifted me up to see him. I thought he was like a monkey with a funny red face, but I did not say anything. I wanted my mother. It was not permitted. Everyone was busy and excited, and I felt lonesome and neglected. I knew it had not been like this when I, second daughter, was born.

When I returned to the living room, our gardener was there in his new coolie coat. It was dark blue with our house name on the collar in white letters. "Honorable master," he said, "I deeply congratulate you on the birth of your first son." Prostrating himself on the hard wooden floor of the corridor to the living room, he bowed his head many times. Aunts and uncles came to offer congratulations. "The foundation of the house is now sound and solid," they repeated again and again. Younger Brother was treated like a treasure from the day of his birth.

When he was two years old, my mother died. It was Boys' Day, on the fifth day of the fifth month, and Younger Brother's streamer was flying high outside the house. I wanted to join him as he reached out toward the streamer from the arms of his maid, but I was held back by the feeling that something unusual was happening. I, four years old, knew nothing of death. Mysterious death had no connection with Mother, lying so quiet, covered with silken spread as if she were alive. But Elder Sister was crying uncontrollably, leaning against Grandmother's knee. Grandmother too was sobbing. I stared at them, motionless, then looked again at Mother's face as she lay so still, her eyes closed, her lovely white hands crossed on her chest. Why did she not open her eyes and call, "Haru"?

She was young and beautiful. Often she had held me on her lap and said, "I shall love you always." When she was sick I had wanted to lie in her bed, but she had refused me sternly. Much later I knew she died of tuberculosis. Her skin was smooth, and always she had used a sweet-smelling lip pomade, daintily putting the tip of her little finger into a beautifully painted jar, and applying the pomade to the center of her lower lip.

On this day her lips, still tinted in the center, did not move. Her black hair, combed sleek, was spread over the pillow. My heart yearning for her tender love, I searched for some reminder of it. Incense was burning at the head of her bed. I did not like the smell. It kept from me my mother's fine fragrance, and I cried.

On the day of the funeral we were all dressed in white silk kimonos and obi-sashes. We traveled in rickshas to the Buddhist Temple, in solemn procession headed by the coffin with its decorations of gold

11

and silver lotus flowers. My young uncle held me on his knees. People in the street stepped aside to let us pass. I was greatly impressed with the importance of the occasion, and considered myself favored.

The Temple, gloomy-dark after the bright sunshine, had a stale, unpleasant odor. The images of Buddha glowed in faint candlelight. We sat on the floor and listened to the long prayer of the Buddhist priest. Grandmother, sitting beside me, closed her eyes and moved her lips, softly repeating the prayer. I waited impatiently for it to be over.

Our house, after the services, was sorrowful, everyone speechless, walking with heavy steps. The relatives left, and only Grandmother remained. Then suddenly I realized I had no mother, and I was lonely. Elder Sister was sick in bed with the measles, and I missed her counsel. When no one was near, I tiptoed to her room and peeped through the slightly opened paper sliding door. She smiled at me, her face blotchy against the flowered counterpane. Younger Brother, lying beside me at night, lifted his tiny head and said, "I wish that Mother would come back very soon." This made me sadder still, and I cried myself to sleep.

The first day Elder Sister was able to sit up, Grandmother made some red rice. Red rice was eaten only on special occasions, such as a return from a long journey, a graduation, or a recovery from illness. Before we started to eat the rice, Grandmother said, "We must give the first bowl to your mother." She dished some rice into Mother's bowl and reverently

12

placed it in front of the family shrine, in which there was a tablet for Mother.

Every morning Grandmother sat in front of the shrine and burned incense, praying with eyes closed. Whenever we received gifts of candies or cakes, she made us place them in front of the shrine before we ate them. An inedible gift was placed in the shrine for Mother to see. Very often the Buddhist priest came to the house to hold special services and prayers for Mother. He was dressed in a long purple gown, and his head was shaved close. As he prayed, he bowed repeatedly and rang a small wooden gong. At the end of the prayer he said eight or nine times something that sounded to me like, "Save me Amida Buddha, save me Amida Buddha." Then Grandmother and we three children, who had sat quietly behind him, went in turn to the shrine and burned incense.

Several months after Mother's death, Father had a talk with Grandmother. He said that he understood her devotion to his children, but that now he released her from the care of them. "My children are growing up in a new age," he said. "I must educate them so that they can meet its challenge with knowledge. Many of the old customs are no longer useful."

Grandmother said in a resigned voice, "So let it be."

When we knew that she was leaving, we implored Father to let us go with her, but he said sternly, "This is your home. This is where you stay."

After Grandmother departed, the family shrine was put away in a closet and not even dusted for many years to come. The priest never again appeared.

13

Father forbade us to offer food or gifts, or to burn incense for Mother. He explained that once a person dies, he turns to earth and has no use for these things. He did not believe in spirits. He never went to Mother's grave and never talked about her. We thought he had forgotten her and we must refrain from mentioning her in his presence. It was not until many years later that we discovered how much Father really loved and missed our mother.

My Father

FATHER WAS a college professor. An intellectual and a scientist, he was full of the contradictions of all enlightened Japan. He believed firmly in the charter oath of the Emperor Meiji, "that harmful customs must be abolished and that knowledge of the entire world shall be sought." He believed just as firmly that only the educated few were qualified to interpret a changing world and to know which were the harmful customs. He tried to reconcile science with superstition by explaining in reasonable terms the wisdom of the old rules, and by giving them a scientific basis. Where a scientific explanation was untenable, he passed off the matter as a law of nature.

Much of Father's spirit of inquiry stopped at his own front gate. His home was to him a background where elaborate rules of Japanese etiquette, the signs

15

of good breeding, had to be observed. In his home he was master, to be respected and revered. I obeyed and honored him; but my docile nature was better able to appreciate the established world of my grandmother than to puzzle about a world in which motion never stood still long enough for me to meditate about it.

Father's jinrikisha, pulling into the gate, made a crunching sound on the graveled path. The jinrikiman called, *"Okaeri!* Your master has come back!" and all the members of the household rushed to the front *genkan* to greet him. The servants halted their work. We all knelt and bowed our heads as he came through the door. This ceremony was a routine which we went through twice a day, when Father left the house in the morning and when he returned in the evening.

Occasionally Father returned on foot and came in without warning through the servants' entrance. The first one who saw him announced loudly, "Your master has come back!" and at the same moment squatted on the floor and bowed. The rest of the family rushed to the back entrance in confusion. Sometimes Father entered before we all were assembled. Then we dropped anywhere in the room, before he passed.

The large and spacious *genkan,* the main entrance, was reserved for Father and for guests. The rest of the family used the side *genkan,* which was smaller and always cluttered with geta, or clogs. We girls were told to keep our geta in orderly manner or no one would want us for brides.

Father changed from Western clothes to long kimono as soon as he returned home. Then he sat on

16

his large special cushion and sipped his tea. When the tea was to his taste, he lingered over it. In the dining room there was always hot water boiling on the *hibachi*. When guests arrived, tea was served to them immediately, even before they were formally received by Father. During their stay their cups were frequently refilled. We had been disciplined to be very quiet while guests were in the house. Even our quarrels were restrained in tone. Sometimes when a guest stayed so long that we had to wait supper for Father, we turned the brooms upside down, believing this would chase guests out.

With supper, Father occasionally had sake wine. This was served warm, and he enjoyed it slowly. His face grew red, and we would receive his attention. With the wine he had *sashimi*, a plate of raw tuna fish decorated with white radish sliced fine and a carrot cut in flower-shape with a piece of green horseradish in the center. We all admired this attractive dainty, but never said anything about its being served only to Father.

Quite unexpectedly there appeared in our dining room an enormous table and chairs. Placed under it to protect the *tatami*-mat flooring was a deep-piled rug. Father said sitting on the floor with our legs under us was bad for our health and posture. Although we liked the novelty of the table, Younger Brother and I could scarcely see over the top, and we found it impossible to manipulate our chopsticks properly. Soon we knelt on our chairs in order to eat in greater comfort. The maid sat on the floor as usual and was embarrassed every time she had to jump up and travel the length of the long table to replenish our rice bowls. The table soon disorganized the entire household. The maids did much grumbling. It interfered with their cleaning, they said, and they bumped against its sides. The rug kept curling up and tripping them. A short time later, just as unexpectedly, the table disappeared. Father said Japanese girls must be trained to sit on the floor. The table found a place in his study, as supplement to his desk.

On the wall in the dining room hung a large map of the world, and often after dinner Father pointed to the pretty pink of Japan, to the soft green of China, and across the wide expanse of blue to the yellow of the United States. He discussed the different customs in these and other countries. It became a game for us to find New York, London, Paris, Berlin, and other cities on the map.

In the spring of my sixth year I entered elementary school which Elder Sister already was attending. Father, with fearsome pride, followed our educational development. When he took trips away from home, he corrected with red ink the letters we wrote him, and sent them back to us. To facilitate our learning the many Japanese characters, he had us keep diaries. Elder Sister and I were to receive a sound education —Father never let us forget it—so as to become better wives and wiser mothers. In tending to our studies we were not to forget our gentleness as women. Man remained woman's superior. "It is an incontestable biological law," said Father, "which keeps woman

18

tied to her home." He esteemed his son more than his daughters, for by natural superiority his son would carry on the destiny of the house; his daughters would be given away as brides and would then belong wholly to their husbands' families.

Father was near-sighted and wore glasses. He said that as a youth he had pored over his books, even closing the outer shutters during the day and studying by lamplight so as not to be disturbed. Much of his reading was in English and German, and he said he had strained his eyes by picking out the tiny letters in these languages. In spite of this he started our study of English at an early age. He drew big letters of the alphabet in black brush ink on large papers and hung them around the playroom walls. To me they looked like bits of wire twisted in fantastic shapes. We repeated each letter after Father, and soon were able to rattle off the A B C's. But when he asked us to begin at the other end, that was not so easy.

Our school reports Father scanned carefully, and when they pleased him, he rewarded us by little excursions on the Day of the Sun, which was a school but not a business holiday.

Throughout my schooldays, I did well in everything but singing. When called upon to sing alone before the class, I was unhappy and did poorly; but at home I sang loudly, trying to imitate the beautiful voice of Elder Sister, who laughed at my efforts. Speaking before the class also frightened me. When it was my turn to stand on the platform, I forgot the stories I knew so well and stared blankly at the blurred faces before

19

me. The teacher said, "You are good in mathematics, composition and penmanship, but you are so shy when you have to speak before the class. But since you will not be a public performer when you grow up, I will excuse you." Once I received a less than perfect rating in sewing. Since sewing was one of the most important womanly arts, I was mortified when I handed my report to Father. To my surprise he made no comment, and took me as well as Elder Sister on our first trip to Asakusa Park.

On such occasions Father had us wear our Western clothes. Elder Sister was especially pleased because of her new high-buttoned shoes. Not so with me. I would have preferred the colorful long-sleeved kimono that most of the other children were wearing, and the thick wooden geta with bells attached that made a happy tinkle as they walked.

Asakusa Park is a noisy amusement park located in the heart of Tokyo. The less-favored of Tokyo's five million inhabitants found the park a welcome release from the tense life of their crowded city. After riding on the street car an hour and changing cars twice, we reached the entrance and were drawn into a swirl of merrymakers. Souvenir and amusement booths lined the pathway, and the crying of hawkers and the gaiety of people was like the buzzing of a million bees. I could hardly tear myself away from the marionette show, in which a girl in pink tights, her cheeks and lips heavily painted, danced on a huge ball.

Carried along by the crowd, we arrived at an open space, where I could again breathe easily. Here was

Kannon Temple, the Temple of the Goddess of Mercy. Old women holding children's hands were resting on the few available benches. Pigeons flew down from the roof to be fed from our hands. A continuous procession of people climbed the stairs leading to the Temple, rang the gong by pulling on a heavy rope of twisted red and white cotton cloth, prayed for a moment, then slipped offerings into one of the many slots in a large padlocked box. It was said that at least a million yen was deposited in the box each year, in the hope that the Goddess of Mercy would deal kindly with the givers. Elder Sister and I took turns at pulling the thick rope with both hands, but the gong made only a feeble sound. Peering into the dim interior, we distinguished the figure of the Kannon sitting far back at the end of the Temple.

We went next to the famous Twelve Story Tower, the highest in Japan, and climbed the spiral staircase to the very top. My head whirled dizzily, and I had to brace myself before I could look over the panoramic view below. Sumida River shone like a silver cord crawling and winding through rows of toy houses. On the other side of the river, black smoke curled thick from many factory chimneys. Spacious Uyeno Park was like a small green hill covered with miniature trees, out of which peeked the vermilion top of Gojuno Pagoda.

On solid ground again, wide-eyed I gazed at the posters outside the theaters. Names of actors were dyed white in big characters on bright-colored streamers strung from poles. With five or six such poles each

21

theater beckoned to the sightseers, irresistibly. Father explained that the entertainment in these theaters was of a cheap variety and not suited for young children. We never questioned his authority, but it was with heart-heavy sense of missing something that we watched other children with their parents disappear inside.

For our next trip, Father suggested Hibiya Park with its hills and wide lawns. Here where the crowds were more leisurely, Elder Sister could promenade and display her Western clothes to advantage. We walked hand in hand, conscious of admiring glances from the onlookers; but I felt that the attentions of all were centered on the beautiful long feather in Elder Sister's white hat, which shook in greeting as she walked.

Once on the Day of the Sun we were taken to a new department store of six stories, the highest in Tokyo at that time. People entering it had to remove their geta; and for people like us, who wore Western shoes, shoe-covers were provided. Father stepped on the escalator which carried people to the first floor, and we, mystified, followed him. My feet slipped, but I grasped the moving belt just in time, and floated upwards. I soon found, to my dismay, that one of the covers was gone from my shoes. Thereafter I tried to be as inconspicuous as possible. When we reached the exit my heart pounded with fear of a rebuke, but the attendant bowed us out silently.

On the other side of the street we entered a stationery store, where, to my joy, no shoe-coverings were necessary. I spied the thousand-year pens and hoped I might have one. But Father purchased long pencils for us, and said, "When you become learned and entitled to a fountain pen, then you shall have one."

Home and Play

OUR HOUSE of two stories was built on a sloping hillside and hidden from view of the street by a stone and wooden fence. From outside the fence one could see only a wave of gray tile on the roof. We lived in a quiet residential section of uptown Tokyo, where other professors and government officials lived. All the houses there were enclosed behind borders of high fence, as if refusing the dust of the street.

Formerly our land had been a woods, and many large maple, bamboo, pine and Gingko trees still remained. I liked the fruit trees best of all. In autumn, with swish of falling leaves the persimmons turned orange-red. The branches were so heavy with the fruit that we thought they would snap. When the persimmons were gone, the chestnuts began to ripen. After a stormy night many of them fell to the ground. I would lie awake listening to the blowing sound of the wind, and in the morning hurry outdoors to gather the chestnuts. I wore high clogs in order to walk safely on the wet ground. In winter only the pine trees remained green, spreading their branches in austere dignity among the naked winter trees. Then the pool beyond the garden was covered to keep the water from freezing. Bamboo sticks were placed over it, and on them were stretched mats with a thick covering of dry pine needles. The pool, covered, was like a mound in the pine-tree forest. We peeped through a small opening and could see the goldfish lying motionless at the dark bottom of the water. At the breaking of winter frost, the plum blossoms bloomed with delicate fragrance along the branch above the dining room eaves. *Uguisu*-birds with green wings visited the tree, and, hidden by the blossoms, sang beautifully all day. The tall cherry-blossom tree beside the gate bloomed in the spring, its lacy-curtain-flowers hanging low. Soon its white petals danced in the air and fluttered to roof and ground, and we picked up the fallen petals and made them into wreaths.

With summer, purple eggplant and green cucumber ripened in our small vegetable garden. Once, before our handyman Jiya came to us, chrysanthemums and dahlias had bloomed in this plot. Father, who was very fond of chrysanthemums, asked Jiya to cultivate them. But Jiya was a stubborn old farmer who never hesitated to say what he thought, even to the master of the house. "You can't eat flowers," he said to Father. "It's a waste of good land. Let me use just this little patch for vegetables."

25

He was given his way, and he sowed the seeds and placed human manure over the ground as fertilizer. The farmers in Japan always use it for vegetables and rice. As the rear entrance of our house faced the vegetable garden, the servants protested vigorously at the bad odor. Jiya paid no attention to them. "We will have a good vegetable garden next summer," he said.

But the odor became so objectionable that finally Father intervened, explaining that the manure was offensive and unsanitary. Jiya looked at him in bewilderment, but promised that thereafter he would use artificial fertilizer. He walked off mumbling to himself, "What a waste of good excrement! What a waste of good excrement!"

Having been a farmer, Jiya continued his habit of rising when the sun rose in the east. He then proceeded to waken the other servants by knocking at the wooden shutters. Ignoring their objections to being aroused so early, he removed the sliding shutters from the grooves. These shutter-panels were stacked during the day in a closet at the end of the long porch. Later in the morning Jiya removed the rest of the panels, beginning at the far end of the house, and working toward our rooms.

Each morning I was awakened by the *gara-gara* clatter of the panels. Floating in half-sleep, I listened to the sound. When Jiya reached our room, the removal of each shutter sent another shaft of light streaming through the paper sliding screens, until finally the night-heavy room was flooded with light.

26

Each morning the sun made different shadows of hanging branches on the paper screens stretched on latticed frames.

"It is time to get up," Jiya called, and added mischievously, "Your eyes will rot if you sleep late."

I could smell the bean soup cooking in the kitchen while I washed my face. This welcome smell wakened me fully, and I hurried to the dining room before the others. "What is in the bean soup, Kimi?" I would ask. "Not spinach!" I did not like the greenish smell of spinach.

If she answered, "*Wakame*," I was glad. *Wakame* is seaweed of soft blue-green color and has the rich smell of the sea.

In summer our breakfast consisted of this bean soup, steaming hot rice, salted cucumbers and eggplant from the garden. We children were given a raw egg each. It was broken into a small cup, seasoned with sugar, and beaten with a chop stick before we drank it with great relish. As master of the house, Father had an additional dish of cooked vegetables.

I had seen Jiya pour his bean soup over his rice, and I tried to imitate him. Father corrected me: "Little daughter, that is not the proper way to eat your food."

After my breakfast I watched Jiya eat in the servants' room. Three times he refilled his rice bowl, poured bean soup over it, and swallowed it quickly, without chewing. I told him how I had been corrected for doing it. "That is right, honorable little

27

one," he said. "It is bad for your stomach. I must eat this way because I have no teeth."

Jiya told us many stories and brought us many traditions of the farm. While he remained with us, we never failed to observe the star festival on the seventh day of the seventh month. On this eve, Jiya cut two bamboo trees from our garden. One he called male and one female. He placed them on the front porch, where we decorated them with colorful *tanzaku*-strings, narrow strips of paper on which poems were written. A table covered with fruits and vegetables was placed as an offering to the stars between the two bamboos. Gazing up at the stars, we listened to Jiya recite the legend.

"Two stars who were in love with each other lived on either side of the River of Heaven," he said. "They were permitted to meet only once a year, on the seventh day of the seventh month. If it rains that night they cannot meet. The rain is their tears. But if the sky is clear, the two loving stars shine brightly because they are happy, and they promise a good harvest. That is what makes me so happy tonight." Jiya's face shone.

Elder Sister Nobu was very beautiful to me under the bright stars. She recited:

> *On the River of Heaven*
> *At the place of the ferry*
> *The princess cried,*
> *"Oh ferryman make haste across the stream,*
> *My prince comes but once a year."*

28

Softly I repeated the words, pretending that she was the princess.

Younger Brother and I played beautifully together, even though I envied him as the center of the family. But he and Elder Sister were always quarreling. One day they started shrieking and screaming because she wouldn't let him play with her doll. At first I paid no attention because it had happened so often; but after a while I was sorry for Younger Brother so unhappily crying. I gave him my favorite doll and told him he could keep it always, and I played with him the rest of the afternoon.

The next evening, on his return home, Father handed me a box tied with red ribbon. "It is a present for you, little daughter," he smiled.

I was surprised. Never before had I alone received a gift. A rosy-cheeked, golden-haired doll clad in Western dress was sleeping in the box.

"Look! Her eyes are blue!" Elder Sister exclaimed in astonishment when I lifted the doll from the box.

"It is an American doll," Father informed us.

This doll became my most treasured possession. I guarded it tenderly for many years.

For Elder Sister and me, the Doll Festival, on the third day of the third month, was an important occasion. Once, a week before the Festival, I cut my hand on glass when I was playing the role of wife with Younger Brother. I was confined to bed because of the deep cut, and Father said there would be no Festival for us that year. Elder Sister reproached me hotly: "How could you be so foolish as to cut your

29

hand at this time!" My heart was shamed and gloomy.

Elder Sister pleaded with Father: "But the *Ohina-sama* will be unhappy and cry in the storeroom if we do not take them out and decorate them." The *Ohina-sama* dolls are carefully stored away in individual boxes, and taken out only once a year for the Doll Festival. As second daughter I did not have a set of my own, but was permitted to share Elder Sister's.

Father finally relented just one day before the celebration, and, with my right hand in a sling, I happily helped Elder Sister prepare the dolls. We set out the special tiered platform of five steps, and covered it with a scarlet rug. On the top step we reverently placed the Emperor and Empress. Just below we put the stately courtiers and ladies of the court. Beneath these came the five court musicians with their flutes and drums. The fourth step held the lowest rank of the court—the footmen. The last step was reserved for household accessories—beautifully lacquered furniture with gold design, dishes, and other articles. All the dolls were garbed in exact miniature reproduction of the ancient official court dress. Even the material was the same as that used in the official imperial costumes. I wanted to decorate some of my own everyday dolls and place them on the lowest step, but Elder Sister would not permit it. "We cannot have such plain dolls mix with royalty," she said.

In the evening, little girl playmates were invited to join us. Beautifully colored *bonbori* lanterns glowed on the top of the doll platform, casting pink-cherry-blossom color on the faces of the dolls. We sat in front of the platform in hushed reverence and watched the expression of their faces change in the flickering light. The party repast of sweet wine and candy was served to us and to the dolls in the dolls' dishes. We believed that they too partook of the feast.

Younger Brother, the only boy to participate in the festival, did not relish his secondary role on this occasion, and became sullen. Nobu upbraided him. "It is only because of the girls that you are able to have these goodies."

"All right," he said with spirit, "but wait till the boys' festival, then I shall be lord."

When Boys' Day came, on the fifth day of the fifth month, each family set up outside the house a special pole on which was hung a colorful streamer shaped like a fish. Younger Brother, as the only boy in the family, had a streamer twenty feet long. This *Nobori,* or streamer, signifies "swimming against the current no matter how strong and swift." It is supposed to inspire boys to be courageous and to overcome all obstacles.

We watched the beautiful, vari-colored streamers waving against the deep May sky. Younger Brother said with satisfaction, "You girls have no such beautiful streamers." Inside the house was a display of dolls representing house-warriors and heroes of old legends. Younger Brother also had miniature swords and bows and arrows and a set of armor, and he pretended that he was a stout warrior. Many little boys were invited to join him in the festivities, but we girls were not so honored. Consoling ourselves, we sniffed, "In spite of

31

his show of bravery, Little Brother cries very easily when he is upset."

Nothing exciting ever happened on our quiet street. Not far away, however, was the business section. Here the street was narrow and crowded with small stores. Wedged in between the fish, meat, and vegetable shops were the crowded ugly shacks of the poor.

Here dull-scaled fish were displayed in large open dishes, lifelessly floating in stale water mixed with blood. We held our noses whenever we passed by. The public bathhouse with thick smoke puffing steadily from black chimneys was next to the vegetable store. Frequently we met people with red-shiny faces, coming out with their soap, swinging their wet bath towels cheerfully. The most popular shop was the one which sold sweet potatoes. Here customers were always waiting for the potatoes to be removed from the large round iron oven. When the heavy wooden cover was lifted, thick white steam carried with it the sweet scent of the potatoes, and customers rushed to buy them.

Children played marbles and jacks in the middle of the street. Young girls of ten or eleven carried a little sister or brother tied on their backs. The infants' pinkish arms and legs flapped, and they pulled their sisters' hair. Housewives with their sleeves tucked back chatted loudly with one another. Their voices were drowned out by the bell of the bean peddler, who was dressed in long tight cotton trousers and had a towel wound around his head. The sweetened boiled beans he carried in two wooden buckets suspended

32

from either end of a bamboo stick. Between peals of the bell he cried, "Hot steaming beans! Hot steaming beans!"

The tofu, or bean curd, peddler always blew a horn to announce his appearance. He too carried his buckets on a bamboo pole, and tofu floated in the water in the buckets. I was told the story that the man who made tofu took a bath in the same tub every night, and for some time I was unable to eat tofu although I was very fond of it.

A clog repairer, a tinsmith, and an umbrella mender came along the street, each calling his trade in his own noisy fashion. The ragman, by contrast, had a droll and sleepy voice. The large basket on his back accepted everything as merchandise, even old papers and broken bottles.

For children, the really popular vendors were the *Ame-uri*. These traveled in couples and sold candies and lollipops formed into colored birds and animals. Now one of these *chindonya* couples came down the street. Bells and drums which they played sounded *"Chin don, chin don."* The woman's outer kimono skirt was tucked up, showing her red petticoat. The man wore white leggings underneath his kimono. Each one balanced a large, shallow wooden washtub filled with candy on his head. The brass rims of the tubs flashed in bright sunshine. Around the rims waved many-colored little flags. Beating drums which hung from their shoulders, the man and woman danced along in perfect step while we children followed excitedly close behind. We were awe-struck that they could balance the tubs on their heads without holding them.

When a crowd of children had gathered, the couple stopped, and the man began, "Welcome, children. Today we have brought a special treat for you. Only a penny each!" He rolled his drum, and the woman started to sing in high-pitched voice. Her make-up showed that at one time she had been a country entertainer. Her partner began to sing with her in his deep voice. High voice and low voice rolled between them like a ball. When their song was finished and a much larger crowd, including many adults, had gathered, the man again beat his drum and announced: "Welcome again! See what I have brought you. With each purchase of candy one of these lovely little flags will be given free." He pulled out a red flag.

A little girl rushed from the crowd with short hurrying steps, and returned with a flag in her hand and a red lollipop-bird in her mouth. Many more children rushed forward like sparrows. Some tugged at their mothers' skirts, pleading for pennies; others ran home to see if they could get a penny there. In a few minutes most of the children were busy licking candy and holding flags proudly. The unfortunate ones stood by, greedily chewing their fingers.

Elder Sister and I watched the performance with no thought of purchasing the candy, which we had been taught was unsanitary. In addition, it was bad manners to ask for money, or to buy candy on the street. But secretly I wondered what the candy tasted like.

I memorized the song which the woman sang, and

back at home I dramatized it with Younger Brother. I placed a cushion on my head. Younger Brother beat the drum. I sang the song of the tragic experience of a girl who dared to fall in love. Just as we were in the midst of this intense scene, Father arrived home and stood horrified. Hastily I dropped the cushion and made a low bow.

Father said severely, "What is this? Does my little daughter imitate street performers and sing undignified songs?"

After that we were no longer permitted to see the *chindonya*. I stood at the front gate every afternoon, hoping that sometime they would pass our house, but all I could hear was the familiar sound in the distance, "*Chin don, chin don.*" They never came along our quiet street.

Second Mother

ONE COLD and dreary winter night I lay awake listening lonesomely to the blind masseur playing a melancholy tune on his flute. Suddenly fire bells rang out clear. I grasped Elder Sister's hand in terror. We knew that if a fire had started in the crowded section it would spread quickly, destroying completely the inflammable wood and paper houses. We knew that we were safe from its cruel onslaught, but we lay awake most of that night, trembling at the thought of the havoc it was bringing.

After that fear-shadowed night we no longer wanted to sleep in our own bedroom, which was in the far wing of the house. Father slept upstairs, on the opposite side of the house. We asked if we might change to the dining room, since it was in the exact center of the house and we could hear walking and voices if we were there. At first Father would not consent, but our persistent and polite pleading won his permission to change temporarily. The maid declared that our sleeping in the dining room would interfere with the proper serving of breakfast. Finally it was decided that we would eat breakfast in the small room next to the kitchen; and Elder Sister, who usually disliked household tasks, gladly helped each evening with the moving of our bedding from our room to the dining room.

One night while we were sleeping there, I awoke suddenly. Thin light from the living room leaked into the darkness between the sliding screens, and I heard Father talking to someone in a whisper. Then a woman spoke: "I quite understand the way you feel, but it is very difficult for a man to take care of three children alone. They need a mother, *ne.**"

My ears pricked up to catch carefully the rest of the conversation which was about us.

Father was silent and the woman continued: "I observed her with her sister's little children, who are about the same ages as yours, and I found her both able and tender. I therefore thought she would make an ideal mother for your children."

There was silence for a while; then Father's voice came hesitatingly through the thin paper wall, "Of course I would like a good mother for my children, but—" He stopped.

* The Japanese *ne* is roughly equivalent to the French *n'est ce pas.*

Again the woman's low voice: "I realize you wish time to make a decision, but I am sure that no more suitable person can be found. Though she is twenty-eight years old, there is nothing wrong with her. She is a sewing teacher in a high school. Her younger sister married before her, and she lost her chance. I can recommend her whole-heartedly as an ideal wife for you."

My heart beat wildly, and I tried to hear more; but the voices became indistinct and soon I fell asleep. Next morning I wondered whether I had actually heard this conversation which was like conversation in a dream. Not knowing, I did not share it with Elder Sister. It would have been impertinent to ask Father, so my heart pondered it all alone.

A short time afterward, Father announced that soon we would have a mother again. Younger Brother, on hearing the news, ran through the house calling, "At last Mother is coming back!"

A large celebration was held to welcome new mother to our house. The sliding paper screens between the dining room and living room and drawing room were taken away, to make one large room of three. Elder Sister and I, dressed in our best kimonos, sat at rigid attention, staring at the strange faces of the many guests. Father and new Mother were close beside me. Since the bride was marrying a widower, she was dressed in sober kimono, trimmed with the white collar of the under-kimono; she wore neither flowers nor other ornaments in her hair. Her severe dress called attention to the diamond in her ring as she rested her white hand on her knee. I studied her glimpsingly, and my impression was favorable. I would have liked to gaze at her longer, but I could not do so without twisting.

Individual red-lacquered tables about a foot high, laden, as was customary, with all the courses at once, were placed before the guests. We children received exactly the same food as the others. This was a formal dinner, and consisted of delicacies of "mountain and sea" served in porcelain bowls and plates. While the warmed sake was being poured for the guests, I lifted my lacquered cup with both hands, pretending that I too had wine. In the excitement, the cup dropped from my hands, hit the corner of my table, and noisily rolled over to where Elder Sister was sitting. She began to giggle. She tried to control herself by placing her long wide sleeve over her lips, but still queer sounds continued. My cheeks burned. Had I ruined my performance before new Mother and all the guests? Indignant at Elder Sister for laughing at me, I hung my head. When I finally raised it, I was relieved to see that no one seemed to have noticed my mishap. I quivered lest Father mention it after the feast, but it was to Elder Sister he directed his reprimand: "It is unbecoming for my daughter to forget her dignity before guests."

The next morning I was playing in the playroom with a multi-colored paper balloon. It jumped up and down on my palm with a *pong-pong* sound, and its colors made a beautiful design as it floated in the air. I was following it with my eyes when I heard my

39

name called. Startled, I dropped the balloon and stood without saying a word. Someone bent down, picked up the balloon, and threw it to me. I caught it mechanically. She smiled encouragingly, and I, flattered by the attention, threw it back to her. Then I realized that this was not just another guest, but a member of the household—my new mother.

Second Mother soon submerged herself in the exacting duties of Father's household. She submitted with strict obedience to carrying out Father's wishes. This was accepted as a matter of course; but so submissively did she discharge her duties that even in the internal affairs of the house, which she was supposed to control, she did not emerge as a real person. With patient tenseness she applied herself almost grimly to warding off that deadly bugbear of a Japanese wife— failure in fulfilling her obligations. Though she later bore my father two children, she feared to show any sentiment toward them lest it be misconstrued as favoritism. She was not well after their births, and wet nurses were employed to look after them.

She was very kind to Elder Sister and me, but Younger Brother was her favorite. On his first day of school she attired him in a new outfit she had made, and accompanied him to the school. Upon his return home she had him photographed in the front entrance of the house. A special feast celebrated this important event.

After new Mother's arrival, heat, electricity, a telephone, and a phonograph were installed in our house. Father always welcomed new conveniences from the

40

Western World. Our house was one of the first to have gas-heating stoves. Father explained to his guests, after they had overcome their astonishment at "the water pipes," that to suffer inconvenience in an industrial age was foolish and not in keeping with the growing spirit of progress. When our gas-light was replaced by electricity, we were thrilled at being able to produce light by a twist of a switch. The advent of the telephone enhanced our prestige in the neighborhood. It was a rare and expensive instrument, and rightly regarded as a treasure. It seldom rang, but when it did, poor Kimi bowed before it and always bumped her head. It was useless to tell her it wasn't necessary to bow; she insisted that it was her duty to pay respect to the spirit of the unseen.

It was the phonograph that gave us the most pleasure. When it was delivered, everyone ceased work and gathered in the living room to scrutinize and hear this wonder. The box was small, with a large horn. Father wound it up slowly, stopping every few turns to look at our awed faces. He inserted the needle deliberately, and put on a record. We held our breaths and sat motionless until the record was finished.

Father was pleased at the reception given the new machine, and asked us to choose the kinds of records we wanted. Elder Sister was in favor of Western operas, while Mother, supported by the maids, preferred Japanese classic music. Younger Brother asked for military marches, and I wanted children's songs. It was not long before the Western music predominated, for Elder Sister practically monopolized the phono-

41

graph. She practiced every day the soprano and coloratura voices. I laughed and clapped my hands when she held her throat and pulled the flesh in and out to make her voice tremble.

One evening Father announced that an English teacher would come to the house once a week so that Mother might take up the study of English. She timidly asserted that she was too old to learn anything new. Father assured her that he did not expect her to master the English language; he only wanted her to learn enough so as not to open an English book upside down. I watched Mother during her weekly lesson laboriously picking out large letters in a child's picture book.

After school one rainy afternoon, when Mother was attending a domestic science class where Father had suggested she might learn Western cooking, I settled myself comfortably with a magazine. Thumbing it through, I was annoyed to find some sewed-up pages. This had happened many times since the day Mother had looked at a magazine which Nobu had borrowed from one of the girls at school. Mother had prevailed upon us to tell her what magazines we wanted, since she would be happy to buy them for us. She bought them, but always censored them before we saw them. This time I decided to find out what the sewed-up pages contained.

Carefully, so as to be able to replace it, I pulled out the cotton thread. Hurriedly and with a nervous feeling of guilt, I read the story. It was about a cruel stepmother, but I did not connect it with my new mother.

42

I could not understand why she had sewed up the pages. My heart felt chagrined at having been dishonorable for so uninteresting a story.

Mother had brought with her a sewing machine finished in shiny-black lacquer. When I first heard its hum, I left my play and hurried to the room where Mother was working. In the diffused light she somehow looked different. Her face was aglow, her eyes glistened, as steadily she directed the material through the hopping needle. I stood entranced, watching her whole body respond to the rhythm. It was as if I watched the freed spirit of a goddess.

When she completed the sewing, she examined it critically, and became aware of my fascinated interest. She showed me then the miniature kimonos and other garments which she kept in a drawer and used as patterns. Mother seldom left the house. In her spare time she escaped to her sewing. She kept the precious machine cleanly dusted and shining. I too respected it, and warned Younger Brother not to touch it.

Sometime later I summoned up enough courage to ask, "My honorable Mother, may I have little pieces of cloth and learn to sew on the machine?" Soon, under her guidance, I was able to make kimonos for my dolls.

She had brought many kimonos with her and she kept making new ones, but she always wore the old ones. On airing day, when she spread them all out to air, I ran my hand gently over the smooth silk. They were dark in color, but they had beautiful linings of

43

red, and trimmings of purple and green. I got my best kimono and laid it beside hers, thinking that if I were a grownup like my honorable mother and had such lovely kimonos, I would wear them every day.

New Year's

"HOW MANY days before the New Year?" Each night as I went to bed I asked the question, putting down another finger for the passage of the day.

This was the liveliest time of the whole year. In Japan, one is a year older at the beginning of the New Year, regardless of the day of birth. I was born in September, but when New Year's came I was already two years old. A Japanese baby is considered one year old at birth.

As the festive time approached, the appearance of our street was changed. The *Kadomatsu,* or pine decoration, was set up before each gate. It was made of pine tree and long bamboo trunk bound together, the pine signifying hardiness and long life, the bamboo virtue and steadfastness. In the business section the streets were full of shoppers. On the sidewalk in front

45

of shop windows, men were busy pounding out dough in a large wooden mixing bowl, in preparation for the holiday supply of *O-mochi,* a kind of special rice patty.

At home I hated to go to bed early. The whole house had to be re-done, clothes put in order, and bills paid, so that the new year could truly begin with a clean slate. On New Year's Eve each room was given a final sweeping, for sweeping the house on New Year's Day would mean sweeping out the God of Fortune. The sacred *Shimenawa*-straw was hung outside of every entrance to keep out the God of Devils.

At midnight the bell of New Year's Eve rang in the Buddhist temple near our house. For many years I had wanted to stay awake and hear it, but not until this year, my ninth, was I permitted to do so. The long vibrating sound rumbled into the night, and its reverberations seemed not to die away but slowly to recede, farther and farther away in the distance.

In the morning the whole family arose before sunrise and dressed in formal style. Father donned his habutai-silk kimono, with loose silk trousers and a crested gown. Younger Brother was dressed exactly like him. Elder Sister and I wore long-sleeved kimonos with broad heavy obi tied behind. We were uncomfortable, but happy to wear these clothes. We gathered in the drawing room and exchanged the formal New Year's greetings. Kneeling on the *tatami-*mat on the floor, I solemnly bowed my head, and pressing my hands on the floor I said, "Honorable Father, congratulations on the New Year." Father acknowledged the greeting with a nod. After the salu-

46

tations were over, we seated ourselves on the cushions and were served the special New Year's dinner.

Behind Father was the Tokonoma, an exquisite alcove, the most prized place in a Japanese room. In the Tokonoma hung the special New Year's scroll. It was made of white silk mounted on gold tapestry; pine tree, bamboo and plum blossom were painted on it, and in the upper corners was a Chinese poem (Japanese culture originally came from China) wishing everyone a happy and peaceful New Year. This scroll had been handed down from our remote ancestors, and had been painted by a famous Japanese artist.

On the Tokonoma stood a square tray holding deep green seaweed, white round rice patty, a red lobster, and a *dai-dai* orange. The lobster was the symbol of long life, of living long enough to have one's back bent like a lobster's; the bitter orange signified a generation.

Father and Younger Brother sat on their cushions in front of the Tokonoma; Mother, Elder Sister and I faced them. The serving maid entered to pour the wine which opened the New Year ceremony. First she offered the red, shallow, lacquered wine-bowl to Father. He held it in both hands and drained it. Then, pouring a few drops into it, she handed it to Younger Brother, next in rank. Mother came next, then Nobu, and then I, sitting stiffly waiting for my share.

The sun was rising when the individual *ozen*-trays were placed before us. On the trays was the traditional New Year's dinner. *Kinton,* sweet chestnuts

47

mashed into sweet potatoes, was served on the same porcelain plate as *Kamaboko,* fish paste with bright red crust. *Funa,* silver carp, was served head and all on a dish of its own. *Kobumaki,* rolled seaweed of deep translucent green, was tied with a thin yellow strip cut from the peel of squash. In the center of the tray was a small round bowl holding a salad of thin strips of carrots and turnips. At one side was a small bowl of orange caviar, and opposite it was the soup containing *O-mochi,* in a lacquered bowl. This was covered by another bowl decorated with the crest of the house.

I liked all the food, but I liked *Kinton* best, so I saved it for last. Elder Sister, noticing this, said, "Haru, you have not eaten your *Kinton.* Will you exchange it for my caviar? I do not like caviar."

"Honorable sister," I said, "you ate up all your *Kinton.* I like it too, but I am saving mine for the end. And you must eat your caviar or you cannot bear children. Kimi told me that if I ate up all my caviar I would have a thousand babies."

"I don't like caviar, and I won't eat it even if I don't have any babies."

Father interrupted, "It won't keep you from having children if you do not eat caviar on New Year's Day. That is merely superstition. Since caviar is eggs of the fish, it is simply a symbol of beginning life. It is a reminder to Japanese women to bear as many children as they can. I am pleased, Haru, that you wish many children when you grow up. But eat your caviar, Nobu. It will help you digest your *O-mochi.*"

48

"You see, honorable sister," I said, "Father advises you to eat your caviar. I will not exchange it for my *Kinton*."

Mother, who had been silent until now, placed her chopsticks on her tray and said, "Haru and Nobu, today is the New Year, a sacred day. Be nice to each other, and do not engage in argument. If you quarrel on the sacred New Year's Day, you will quarrel throughout the year."

Father turned his attention to Younger Brother, who was flushed with having eaten so much food. He said, "Soon you will start school. You are old enough to make a New Year's resolution."

Elder Sister broke in, "Honorable Father, I have made my New Year's resolutions. I shall not tease my brother any more, and I shall write in my diary every day."

"That is excellent, Nobu," Father said. "We must try to overcome our faults in the New Year, but it is also proper to determine on some new accomplishment."

"Honorable Father," said Younger Brother, "when I grow up I want to be a brave general. And wear lots of decorations."

"Then, Taro," Father said, "you must also resolve not to fear the dark."

He beamed at his son, then looked at us. "I shall reveal to you my resolution," he said. "This year I resolve to go to Germany to study."

I looked at Father in awe. To go abroad—that was what I would like, too. Perhaps if I became learned

49

like Father I could go to foreign countries some day. I determined to study diligently, but I did not voice my resolve.

Father did not realize his goal that year or for many years, for the following summer the World War broke out, and Japan took her stand on the side of the Allies.

After the feast Elder Sister Nobu and I quickly changed from formal clothes to ceremonial school kimono. Although we had a two weeks' holiday, we had to attend a special assembly on this day to be reminded of our national duties. The principal made his customary short speech, telling us of our good fortune in being under the protection of the Emperor. He said that affirming our love for the Emperor and our loyalty to his reign would keep us from harm throughout the year.

When I returned home, Younger Brother was flying his kite. The kite was bigger than he was, and had a picture of a warrior painted on it. We girls played badminton with beautifully painted *Hagoita*-rackets for the rest of the afternoon. In the evening we played the *Hyakunin-Isshu*, poetry games. From my earliest years I had memorized many poems, most of which I did not understand. In these games, cards were dealt to all the players, who placed them on the *tatami* floor in front of them. One person recited the first few lines of a poem, and the first player to recognize the remaining lines on his own card won the game. Father, who had a good voice, was usually the reader. The verses were old and beautiful. One of my favorites was:

50

The peaceful spring day
With the sun beaming far away,
Why must blossoms fly
With calmless heart . . .
—Kino Motonori

During the week of New Year's festivities we visited many friends and relatives, always traveling in the riksha. When we traveled down the slopes at great speed, I held my breath and shut my eyes. On the seventh day the pine decoration was taken away from the gate. I leaned against the gatepost and watched the gardener remove bamboo and pine. Many days would pass before the next New Year.

On the Beach

IN THE SUMMER of 1914, Father decided that we should remain in Tokyo instead of going to the beach where we had gone for many years. We were in mourning for the Empress Dowager who had died a few months before; I was still wearing on my kimono a little black bow such as I had worn all through the year following the Emperor's passing. But as the weather grew more sultry and unbearable, Father saw no good reason for our remaining in town, and he sent my second mother and us children to the beach.

The trip was always a joyous and happy one. Katase beach was not far from Tokyo, only two hours by train. Yet it seemed to us a long journey. Elder Sister and I spent much time selecting the books, toys and hair ribbons to carry with us. Jinrikishas took us and our baggage to the station. On the train we sat near the window so as to look out over the fields as we passed. Through the open window the summer breeze came softly, with lovely scent of fresh grass. The trees in the fields, the electric poles, and the adjoining hills seemed to run faster than the train. Green waves of wheat in a sea of yellow *calza* flowers made a picture like pretty patterned kimonos put out to air. In the distance the fields and hills moved slowly. Farmers in the fields straightened their bent backs and looked at the passing train.

We stayed at the same inn every year and occupied the same quarters. From our room we could see Katase River flowing into the sea. Beyond the river soft hills spread out to the horizon. When the sky was clear, snow-peaked Mount Fuji appeared beyond the sand hills. If at sunset Mount Fuji turned deep purple against the red sky, I would say to Elder Sister, "Tomorrow will be a nice day."

Before breakfast we walked on the beach, collecting shells and seaweed. We washed the seaweed, dried it, and made bookmarks of it. Often on our early morning walks the shell trumpets of fishermen signaled their homecoming from the sea. Then Nobu would say, "Let's watch the fish nets come in."

As we watched, the small gray spot on the horizon grew slowly into ships approaching the shore. The morning mists dispersed, and the bright sun sparkled over the water. The sound of the shell trumpets brought wives and children of the fishermen running to the shore. The women wore short white garments

53

which exposed their legs and thighs. They were bare-
footed, as were the dark-faced children, and they left
a design of footprints behind them in the washed
sand.

Low bass voices greeted the women and children
as the boats drew near. One by one the fishermen
stepped into the water, where the women were waiting to welcome them. Men and women lined up together to haul in the heavy nets. The copper-brown
skin of the fishermen was emphasized by the strips
of white or red cloth covering their loins. Men, women
and children chanted the song of the fisherman,
"*Eiyara ye-e-e Yotto Ko-Sho-o-o,*" the rhythm of the
chant meeting the rise and fall of the waves. When
the heavily burdened net was pulled onto the sand
and the silver and blue-scaled fish jumped vigorously
inside it, they all shouted with joy. Each of the children received a few fish for his part in the task, and
ran off noisily, holding the fish by the tails.

These children were all familiar to us, but we never
exchanged greetings with them. When we met them
face to face, we never smiled, but only returned their
expressionless stares. We would meet them again in
the hot afternoons when everyone went swimming.
The boys swam naked and like fish behind the rocks.
The girls in their cotton garments swam with us.
Their garments clung to them when they emerged
from the water, and we thought that they looked long-
ingly at our pretty bathing suits. Two or three years
later we were surprised to see these same fishermen's
daughters working in souvenir shops in the business

street and acting quite grown-up. Also in the back
section of the town I saw some of them, my own age,
sweeping and washing stairways and doing other
menial work around hotels and inns. I could not understand why they had gone from childhood to womanhood without, like us, passing through a period
of girlhood.

After swimming we usually had cold drinks at the
refreshment stand. We wished that Father would visit
us, for then we would have special *chikara-mochi*
cakes with syrup poured over them. We knew that
this summer Father would be particularly happy because Younger Brother had learned to swim.

But Father visited us only once, late in August.
We sat on the beach eating our cakes, and Father
read his newspaper. His face looked tired as he read.
Suddenly he put the paper down and told Mother
in solemn words that an Imperial edict had just been
issued involving Japan in war with the Allied countries.

We all were quiet.

Younger Brother Taro broke the silence with, "I
shall be a general and win the war."

Mother looked at him anxiously, then said in list-
less voice, "Our soldiers fight well."

To me the news had no significance, but with the
others I was silent. Then Younger Brother plunged
into the water, and Father beamed as he exhibited
his swimming skill.

In the twilight the water turned deep dark blue,
and the sky glowed red, purple and orange. After

supper Elder Sister and I strolled on the beach, dressed in gay flowered kimonos with long wide sleeves that danced like butterflies in the wind. We looked at the sea, spreading endlessly before us. Nobu said, "Far away, beyond that horizon is America."

We watched the sea and horizon melt together in dark purple. Out in the distance we saw the faint glimmer of the lighthouse. Beyond this gathering darkness I tried to picture that strange and exotic country, America, filled with blond children eating ice-cream and chocolates. Elder Sister had the same thought. As our faces met in the darkness she said, "I wish we could go to America some day."

Bright stars began to appear in the buoyancy of space. I imagined that I had wings and could fly skyward. What would I find in that fairyland of the sky? The music of the waves washed the shore in appealing song. The soft breeze touched my cheeks, and dreamily I remembered the fairy story of Urashima Taro, which Nobu had read to me when I was very small.

Long, long ago, the story told, there lived a fisherman named Urashima Taro. . . . The story was so familiar to me that I could see Urashima come walking on the beach. . . . One day he saw some children playing with a turtle. Being a kind-hearted man and thinking the poor turtle might be tortured, he bought it from the children and set it free in the sea. The next day, drifting along in his boat, he heard his name called. There on the surface of the water he saw the very turtle which he had freed the previous day. The turtle thanked Urashima for his kindness and invited him to the palace of the sea. The turtle grew and grew till Urashima could sit on its back; and down to the bottom of the sea they dived and reached a palace of coral where beautiful princess Oto-hime, dressed in a golden gown, greeted them with a smile. She told Urashima that he was to be her prince and live with her in the land of eternal youth because he had saved her turtle-emissary. There in the palace of coral with many-jeweled walls, what he thought was three days passed like one moment to Urashima. Then he asked if he could return to his native village to see his parents. The princess said it could be arranged, and, giving him a lacquered box as a token of her love, she said, "This contains something very precious. You are never to open it." When Urashima returned to his native village he found the same hills and the same shore, but all the people were strange. A strange man came to the door of his own home and asked, "Who are you?" When Urashima told him, the stranger said, "Yes, everyone knows the legend of Urashima. I heard it as a child from my grandparents." Slowly Urashima divined that instead of three days he had spent three hundred years in the palace of the sea. In a rash moment he opened the box which the princess had given him. Vapor poured out and covered him, leaving him a very old man, his black hair turned to white. . . .

Lost in dream-pity for Urashima, I was brought back to earth by Elder Sister's voice. "Come on," she said, "everyone is going home." She grabbed my hand

57

and made me run very fast. Urashima, the palace of the sea, and the beautiful princess disappeared in the deep black sea.

We hurried through the pine grove and reached the lighted business street. There, blinking our eyes in the unaccustomed light, we slowed our hastening steps to a well-bred saunter.

In the early fall we returned to Tokyo. As we passed huts, trees, fields and hills, my heart bade them regretful farewell.

"New Women"

THE CARETAKER of our school passed our house every day. She was short, and she waddled along slowly on her thin flat straw sandals, her back bent, her hands snuggled crosswise into the tight sleeves of her dark blue cotton kimono. When she met us, she smiled, showing her lone tooth. She had a pug nose, a large mouth, and gray hair pulled tight into a bun. At school the children called her "Granny" because even though she was only middle-aged, she looked so old. Her sweeping and dusting and satisfying the teachers' wants and attending children who became ill left her little time to rest in her room, which was a few steps from the main corridor. But sometimes we saw her there, bending over her charcoal stove, blowing white steam off her cup of hot water. She was sweet to the children, and we were all fond of her.

One day just as Elder Sister and I started to school, Granny passed by and bowed to us, smiling as usual. After she was out of earshot, Nobu whispered, "I have heard that Granny lives differently from normal people. While she is at work in the school, her husband stays at home and does the housework and takes care of the children."

I was shocked. What kind of man could this be to stay at home and let his wife go out to work? How could she stand such a life? Did she feel unhappy at the disgrace? I was enraged to think that this kind of woman had such a miserable husband.

Soon after this my teacher told us about the "new women." "They do not want to stay at home, but wish to go out and work just as men do," she said.

Immediately I thought of Granny. Was she a new woman? I could not be sure and finally I asked my teacher. At first she smiled; then her expression changed. "No," she replied, "Granny is not a 'new woman' even though she is working."

Teacher then launched into an attack on women who demanded freedom and equal rights with men. "New women insist that their husbands help them with their wraps and carry their parcels just because they do it for the men," she said. "If Japanese women lose their gentleness and obedience, they will soon become base and useless creatures. These new women go to Yoshiwara (famous red-light district) and drink wine of five different colors. They have 'own-choice'

60

men, called sweethearts, and they walk with them arm in arm. This public display is no better than the love practice of cats and dogs!"

By this time I pictured the new women as demons. I was relieved that Granny was not one of them. At home I asked Kimi whether she had ever heard of the new women. She said that she had, that she knew all about them.

"Do you know," she said, "that they wear cotton kimonos with short sleeves like boys, and also men's overcoats, and that they most improperly walk with men? Why, in my village, even married couples never walk together on the street."

Elder Sister entered the conversation. "These new women all have 'young swallows,'" she said.

I wondered what kind of bird a young swallow was.

Elder Sister laughed at my ignorance and explained, "A young swallow is a husband or sweetheart who is younger than his wife and supported by her."

"Is Granny's husband a young bird?" I wanted to know.

Nobu shrugged her shoulders and laughed again. "An old woman like that cannot have a young swallow. The new women are much younger. They read and write and make speeches. Some of them, Haru, even write novels and other books."

By this time I was quite confused. Teacher, the maid, and Elder Sister all had different definitions of the new woman. I asked Nobu, "Is it proper to admire them—the new women?"

She said that she too was puzzled. I asked my

61

mother about them. She looked thoughtful and said, "I disapprove of women abandoning their feminine customs. Woman's lot is harder than man's, but it is our fate. Only evil can come if we protest against it."

Father voiced his opinion of new women when Elder Sister asked him, "Why are new women called 'blue stocking'? What does it mean?"

He explained: "The name is taken from a similar group of free women who were active in England about a century ago."

My only idea of stockings in the Western World— blue or any other color—was stockings filled with Christmas presents. I could not understand why this symbol should be used.

Father went on: "When I was a young boy, there was a movement among wealthy Japanese women to abandon the kimono entirely and to give social dances where men and women embraced each other to wild music. Soon they gave up this barbarism and returned to the Japanese customs. This time the imitation is less frivolous, but nevertheless Japanese women will soon come back again to their own ways. It is not," he hastened to make himself clear, "that I object to women studying and bettering themselves culturally. But these extreme methods new women are pursuing—leaving their homes, competing with men, mocking their womanhood—these I cannot approve." He looked at us earnestly. "Even though my daughters receive a Western education, I want them to maintain all of a Japanese woman's virtue and charm."

I had almost forgotten about the new women when

62

Elder Sister showed me a picture of a bride in a news-paper. "There," she said, "that is one of the new women."

I was amazed. "Why, this is a beautiful Japanese bride," I said. "She does not look at all like a demon."

End of Childhood

IT WAS LATE in October and the air was chill. Elder Sister and I sat quietly on our cushions, watching Father. He was leaning over the *hibachi* with bent head, and writing on the hot cinders. Quickly he erased what he had written, and absent-mindedly began again. His shadow was cast blackly on the opposite wall, and under the ceiling light I saw the gray hairs on his head. We sat voiceless. Second Mother's cushion was empty. It was one week after her death.

Father at last raised his head and said, half to himself, "This is our fate and we must accept it. Life and death are in the will of heaven. There is no use lamenting endlessly." He rose and asked Elder Sister to serve tea. As we started to sip the tea he took off his eye-glasses, saying that the steam from the tea had blurred them. He wiped his eyes and his glasses

64

with his handkerchief, and assumed a more cheerful expression.

Because of the nature of Second Mother's illness, typhoid fever, we children had not been permitted to visit her at the hospital. She had had to be cremated when she died, and only her ashes had been brought home. I missed her and hated to think that she never would come back, and my thoughts turned to the poor little stepsisters who were about the ages we had been when our own mother died, and to Younger Brother who would most of all miss Second Mother's tender care.

Elder Sister, always so lively and gay, now became quiet and subdued. She took over many responsibilities of the house. She served tea, prepared Father's clothes, and attended to other details reserved for the mistress. One evening when we were sitting in mournful meditation, she went to the storeroom, found the family shrine, dusted it and set it up. She pushed toward the back our ancestors' tablets, and put Mother's and Second Mother's side by side in the front row. She burned incense and murmured, "Namu Amida Buddha, save me Amida Buddha," as we both bowed reverently before the spirits of our departed mothers. I thought Father would forbid it, but apparently he was too desolate to care. When I received a prize from school, I placed it in the front row of the shrine.

Soon after Second Mother's death, all her belongings were removed by her mother. I ached with memories when the men began to carry out the sewing machine. I wanted to pull it from them; it was as though they were carrying out her coffin. I cried bitterly. Elder Sister too was deeply hurt. Had we not been real daughters to our stepmother? Our thoughts turned back to our own mother.

From the storeroom we retrieved our own mother's mirror stand and a small red-lacquered chest of drawers. When Second Mother came to our house, we had been instructed by Father that it was our duty to her not to talk or even to think of our real mother. But now we used her furniture in our room, and our memories of childhood, sunk into darkness, took shape again in light. In the chest of drawers we found embroidery and silk work done by Mother. Once, in a low built-in chest in the drawing room, I found yellow photographs, all of us as very small children, and Mother, and our grandparents whom we had not seen for many years. Best of all the pictures I liked the the one of my mother alone. She was wearing black ceremonial kimono decorated with five crests, and with the white scarf-like edging of the under-kimono contrasting prettily at the neck. She looked very lovely, the touch of lip-rouge in the center of her lower lip bringing out the fragile beauty of her face. Once Elder Sister found an old diary of Father's. "Look at this!" she exclaimed in great excitement. "Father has written a great deal about our mother. He must have been very fond of her." I was happy at this revelation, but distressed that Elder Sister should go through Father's desk and discover secrets.

After my stepmother's death there was no formal

welcome for me when I returned from school. Elder Sister was now attending Girls' High School, some distance from home, and she did not come back until very late in the afternoon. I had many lonely hours. Second Mother, after greeting me warmly, had always prepared afternoon tea and cakes. Now the tea and cakes were the same, but partaking of them was no longer a ceremony. Attracted by laughter and conversation of the servants preparing the evening meal, I went out to the kitchen. But soon I was told, "Honorable daughter must not stay in the kitchen," and was politely ushered out. I wandered restlessly from room to room.

After a period of this lonesome time, a middle-aged woman came to live at our house and take over the duties of housekeeper. Although she was not related to us, we called her Oba-san (Aunt). Father was teaching away from home much of the time, but Oba-san's kindness and attentiveness ended our loneliness. Sometimes she prepared tea for us while we were studying after supper. We liked this change from the clock-like routine of Second Mother. She selected very gay kimonos for us. On shopping tours she took us to a Western restaurant, where we ate awkwardly with knives and forks and large white napkins. One memorable day when Father was away she took us to a theater.

The performance started late in the afternoon, but we began to prepare for it in the early morning. We wore our best kimonos and arranged our hair in Japanese coiffure. We drove to the theater in jinrikisha, and

67

felt really grown-up when we were welcomed by the booming professional greeting of the dignified doorman. The keeper of geta, in dark blue coolie coat, approached and took our geta and handed us in return a board on which was indicated in black ink the check numbers for the clogs. The lobbies and aisles of the theater were covered with deep straw *tatami*-mats. The entire theater was arranged in boxes, except for standing room in the rear. We sat on cushions on the *tatami*. Before curtain time I watched with interest the people coming in, followed by cushion carriers who placed the cushions in their assigned positions.

Soon a gong sounded as signal for silence, and wooden clappers were heard behind stage as the beautiful long curtain of purple and gold design slid slowly to one side. The musicians sat on elevated seats on the left side of the stage. They were dressed in uniforms of dark kimono with stiffly starched *kamishimo* which stood out at the shoulders and came triangularly to the waist.

The play, *Forty-seven Ronin*, was a classic in story as well as dramatic form. Its music was very popular, and since we had a record of it at home, I anticipated enjoying the play very much. But it was acted in classic language, and I was disappointed when I heard the deep voices of the men in women's roles. There are no women performers in Japanese classic plays. The strangeness, the strain of trying to follow the unfamiliar words, made me very sleepy. The voices seemed to come from a distance in a foreign language. My eyelids came closer together, and the music on the stage was a lullaby in a dream. Suddenly it was intermission.

"How did you like the play?" Elder Sister asked. I could not admit that I had fallen asleep and had not understood it, so I answered evasively.

I was fully awake, however, when Oba-san ordered supper from the usher. Soon a waiter came, carrying on the palm of one hand held high over his head several piled-up lacquered boxes. In the other hand he carried a teapot and teacups. We were served in our places, and never did food have so romantic a glow.

This first trip to the theater was the last for many years, for not until we were fully grown-up did Father permit us to go again.

Because of all these things we soon felt very near to Oba-san. It was she who decided that we should go to visit our own mother's parents. We were surprised when one Sunday a servant of our real aunt appeared and invited us to her house, saying that our real grandparents and all the grandchildren would be present. Father was not at home, and Elder Sister, who ordinarily made quick decisions, turned to me for advice. We could not decide whether it would be proper until Oba-san settled it for us. "Go to your grandmother, *ne*," she said. "I am sure it will make her very happy to see you."

Oba-san selected our best kimonos and suggested that Elder Sister powder her face, saying, "You must look your best since your grandmother has not seen you for many years." We spent much time over our

69

toilet, and Oba-san took particular pains with Younger Brother. The servant led the way, and as we walked along I still meditated on the propriety of the trip, since I thought that Father would not have permitted it if he had been at home. "Do you think it is right for us to go without Father's consent?" I asked Elder Sister.

She answered quite definitely this time. "We go to see our stepgrandparents even though our stepmother has died, so why can't we visit our real grandparents?" That reassured me, and I continued with lighter heart.

The walk was a short one, and we were amazed that in all this time we had not been told that our real aunt lived so close to us. Many cousins whom we did not know were already gathered in the house. Grandmother greeted us and exclaimed, "How you've all grown, how you've all grown, *ne!*" She led us to the *hibachi*, and we sat primly on our cushions beside the fire.

Honored Grandfather sat back on his cushion smoking his long pipe and gazing at us as though trying to read what the years had done to us. I looked with respect at his white beard. He had not changed much from the old photographs I had found in the chest.

Elder Sister and I, our knees together, sat in the stiff position we used for guests, and bowed our heads. Grandmother said, "Do not sit so stiffly, *ne*. This is your own home. Come closer," she went on. "These many years I have longed to see my grandchildren, but on several occasions when I tried to see you, your honorable father refused. He said it would upset your nice relationship with your second mother. Whenever I visited Tokyo, I came close to your house, hoping I might hear your voices or see you playing around the gate. I lingered for a while but it was quiet, no voice, no sight of you. I had to content myself with just looking and being thankful that you were protected by a solid roof."

She stopped for a moment as though she feared her voice might break; then she noticed my hands as I warmed them at the *hibachi.* "Your hands are just like your mother's," she said.

She caught her breath and looked at Nobu. "I have long had in mind that the time has come for my granddaughters to turn their thoughts to their future homes. I was already betrothed at your age, Nobu."

We looked at her blankly. Although our training was by no means inimical to such a fate, we thought of it only as something that would follow in the future.

"It is well," Grandmother said, "for a maiden to spend the years of her girlhood preparing for her station as wife. To know her destiny gives her an opportunity to become familiar with the habits of her future family and learn to conform to them. It makes easier the life together later, and centers her thoughts where they should be—on making ready for her husband's position."

Two spots of color struggled through the thick powder on Elder Sister's cheeks, but she cast down her eyes and said nothing. Grandfather spoke to her: "And does my little granddaughter attend high school?"

71

Nobu seemed grateful for the change in conversation and answered softly, "Yes, my honorable Grandfather, I now attend Girls' High School."

"My, my," said Grandmother, "must you travel such a distance? Are there not adequate schools closer home?"

"Yes," Nobu replied. "But this high school is considered the best, and the students are carefully selected. Second Mother was overjoyed when I was accepted. She had worried so much about the disgrace it would have been if I had not passed the examinations."

"We had a big feast afterwards," Younger Brother added.

Grandmother shook her head. "I cannot see of what use higher education is to girls. All these boys' subjects taught in girls' schools—it's against the design of the gods. I hear many disturbing stories of over-educated girls today. But I am glad to see that my granddaughters are modest and gentle and retain their womanly virtues."

Knowing it would please Grandmother, Nobu said, "We have very good classes in manners and ethics, honorable Grandmother."

It meant little either to Grandmother or to us that this was the year 1916, and that a whole world was at war. We did not know that last year China had become incensed at Japan's twenty-one demands; or that a law passed in 1912 had just gone into effect, limiting the workday of children to twelve hours; or that a cry for *minsei, minken* and *jiyu*—popular government, justice, and liberty—was just beginning among the populace. This was all beyond the comprehension of us or of Grandmother. Her world still revolved around her family, her home, her husband, in the way of her ancestors.

"If we stray from the path of our ancestors," she said now, "we shall lose the peace within us. So it was determined in the long, long ago." Then she added, her eyes twinkling, "And now let us partake of the dinner which has been prepared."

The main vegetable dish had bits of shredded chicken in it. Grandmother had never tasted other meat. She said it had a bad smell. This idea about meat originated in the feudal period when it was considered barbaric to eat any animal except chicken. It is said by historians that the custom originated during the rule of Tokuawa, who used this method to keep his subjects meek. We tried to convince Grandmother that she ought to taste meat sometime. "I do not wish to imitate the foreigner," she said.

During dinner Grandmother asked, "And how are your little stepsisters? Be kind to them, since they too are motherless. Next time you come, bring them with you."

I was pleased at this, for our stepgrandparents did not trust our attitude toward our stepsisters, and treated us coolly.

Grandfather delightedly counted all of his grandchildren, and asked each of us to recite something we

73

had learned in school. When my turn came, shyly I
recited in sing-song:

> *On top of the hill in sunset*
> *Leaves of Gingko tree*
> *Fly and scatter*
> *Like tiny golden birds.*
> —Yosano Akiko

PART TWO

Entering Girls' High School

IN 1917, about three months before graduation from the six years of elementary school, I began
preparing for entrance examinations for the same
Girls' High School which Elder Sister was attending.
Every night I studied until the wall clock drowsily
struck nine. The hour of nine was for me the "hour
of the ox," when even the grass and the trees were
sleeping.

At school the pupils who were going to High School
were assembled for special study for the entrance examinations, so that during the short winter days I did
not come home until dusk. We called the examination
period "examination hell" because the competition
was so keen.

Oba-san said that drinking raw eggs would improve the brain, and on the first morning of examina-

77

tion she broke two eggs into a bowl. They tasted peculiar with no seasoning of sugar or soy sauce, but I drank them to the last drop. Then, accompanied by Elder Sister and Oba-san, and carrying a half dozen pencils which had been sharpened the night before, and an eraser and a bundle of paper, I left the house. Even on the streetcar Elder Sister continued my preparation by writing the difficult Chinese characters on my palm with her finger. "Be sure you write the characters very clearly," she cautioned me.

The examination lasted three days. I felt as though my heart shrank and expanded each time I thought of my answers. On the fourth day, when the results were to be announced, I entered the school gate, trusting my luck to heaven. A cherry tree was blooming in pink profusion. I could not help thinking that it had been planted there only that morning. In the schoolyard anxious-faced children held their mothers' hands. Eagerness to know the results of the examination and fear of knowing them were jumbled in my mind. At the appointed time a long paper, listing the numbers of the successful examinees, was pasted on the wall opposite us. Everyone stood before it, leaning forward with neck out-thrust. My heart beat violently and I grasped Nobu's hand.

"My number is 476, you know," I said.

Elder Sister suggested that we start from the top and read the numbers aloud so that we would not skip any number. For a while I read with her; then the closely-written numbers blurred into one mass before my eyes. So I looked at my feet and listened to

Nobu. I felt as though I were being pricked by needles.

"There it is! There it is! 476!"

Half believing, half doubting, I raised my head at Elder Sister's shouting. Looking where she pointed, I saw it. It was not a mistake. I grasped her hand with both of mine and jumped up and down like a rabbit. The dark curtain that had been hanging before my eyes rolled up suddenly, and clear sun-ray fell upon my path. A wide bright plain spread out before me as far as eye could see.

As a reward, Father gave me a thousand-year pen and an English dictionary with a red cover.

The week's spring vacation ended at last, and the morning came when I was to go to the Girls' High School. I put on a long lobster-brown *hakama* over a new cotton kimono with short rounded sleeves. It was the rule of the school that silk could not be worn. Oba-san said that was uneconomical but that if it was the rule it couldn't be helped, and she made the kimono for me. On my hips I wore the school badge, which I had often gazed at enviously on Elder Sister. It was a hexagon of silver and green with a design of pine tree and snow; the latter symbolized mind as pure as snow, the former virtue as high as the pine. In my flowered *furoshiki* I carried the thick High School textbooks with their smell of new paper. They were heavy, but that heaviness was delightful to me. Hastily I put on my shoes, and tried to hurry Elder Sister, who read the paper and said that it was still early. Even the fifty-minute ride to the school in

79

a jolting streetcar was happiness to me. The trolley car and the streets far from home were part of a grown-up world filled with strange things, and my own world seemed suddenly extended.

Girls' High School was a wooden building of Western style. In the auditorium, which held more than a thousand people, was a black veneered piano, its half-open lid exposing white glistening keys. Thin glass-shining test-tubes were ranged in rows in the chemistry laboratory; they whispered to me the mysteries of the universe. The gymnasium contained American apparatus.

Our *hakama* could be opened at the pleats. When we changed the buttoning they became trousers, and when we gathered up the hem with a string, they became bloomers. My legs felt very light during the gym period when we tied up the *hakama*. The teacher boasted that modern girls were taller than their mothers because of Western gymnastics, and so we competed with each other in pulling up our bloomers and making our legs look longer. But the principal reprimanded us, and said that displaying our fat legs showed a lack of womanly modesty. After that I tied my *hakama* just below the knees, although I felt sad about doing it.

Of all the new courses in Girls' High School I liked English the most. The illustrated reader bore to me the fragrance of foreign lands. I, who had learned my A B C's from Father, now kept my English dictionary proudly by my side. The man teacher read to us in a loud voice, and we read after him. No

Japanese word ends in a consonant, and he gave a Japanese pronunciation to the English words by putting a vowel at the end of each of them. Imitating his pronunciation, we repeated in unison: "Itto isu ah catto. Zisu isu ah doggu."

After a while this teacher was replaced by a young woman teacher, a graduate of a mission school, and our pronunciation came somewhat closer to the English. This new teacher was tall and slender, and she wore her hair in the most recent fashion called *joyu-mage*, or actress haircomb. Instead of having the front lock with the padding in it jut out like the visor of a cap, she had her hair parted in the middle and pulled back in a chignon behind the ears. In my heart I liked this beautiful teacher, but her gay clothes and her haircomb were not teacher-like, and I wondered if they were proper. After she came, the upperclass girls, who wore much longer *hakama* than we, began coming to school with their hair in *joyu-mage*. Then one morning, at an assembly of the entire school, the principal forbade this haircomb; it was not to be copied, he said, by daughters of refined families.

In less than a year, however, nearly everyone, regardless of station, was wearing *joyu-mage*. One morning even the ethics teacher came in with her hair combed in this fashion. Involuntarily I strained my eyes to look at her. She was wearing her usual black *hakama*, and her stiff, glum expression had not changed. In Ethics we learned spiritual education for wifehood and motherhood; it was an important course for us, and so when the teacher entered the

81

classroom we bowed especially politely. On this morning, even though her haircomb had changed, we bowed as before, greeting her without a whisper.

We were to study this day the story of General Nogi's wife, and to learn from it the way of Japanese women. Nogi had been a well-known general, famous during the Russo-Japanese War. Younger Brother, thrusting out his chest covered with toy medals and throwing back his shoulders, had always said that he would become as distinguished as General Nogi. About the time I entered elementary school, General Nogi and his wife had followed their master, Emperor Meiji, in death. The General, already the hero of the people, then became a god and was enshrined in Nogi Jinja.

Father opposed this custom of following the master in death. He said, "It is regrettable that we have lost such a loyal subject as General Nogi. It would have been better if he had continued to live and serve the nation." These words remained clearly in my mind as I craned my neck and, half-absorbed in the teacher's new haircomb, listened to her discourse to the class. I felt I could not accept the story without questioning.

Madame General Nogi, clothed in her white silk death robe, had sat quietly in her own room composing her death-poem; then with imperturbable tranquility she had taken her life. The teacher wrote on the blackboard the death-poems of General Nogi and Madame Nogi, and commanded us to memorize them. General Nogi had written:

82

From this mirrored world
His god has withdrawn;
In my great sovereign lord's
August footsteps following,
I too depart.

Madame Nogi's poem was this:

He is gone . . .
From today's Imperial visit
They say there is no return.
I will be sad
To meet Him today.

"Worthy of a warrior's wife!" the teacher said. "The resolution to share death with her husband was a noble one. With just one thrust of the dagger she pierced her heart and achieved a beautiful end."

I felt a little sad. Must a fine wife share death as well as life with her husband?

The teacher went on, "Even before death she was tranquility itself. She had the profundity of the Japanese woman who, enfolding deep within her heart sorrow, suffering, and joy, shows it neither in face nor in words. Although a woman, she sacrificed her two sons for the nation during the Russo-Japanese War. For a mother there is no greater honor than this. Madame Nogi is indeed the mirror of Woman."

The teacher's words sounded far away as my mind wandered to other thoughts. General Nogi had been intensely grieved at the great loss of life among his soldiers during the siege of Port Arthur. In the same

83

battle the General had lost his own two sons. Perhaps
for these reasons he had chosen death when con-
fronted with the death of the Emperor Meiji whom he
had served all his life. . . . In Madame General's
heart lay hidden the sorrow of a mother who had lost
her children. For the first time Madame Nogi as a person touched my heart. . . .

Another course, as valuable as Ethics, was Conduct, in which we learned gentle, womanly deport-
ment. The conduct room was of pure Japanese style,
removed from the Western-style building, and facing
a small garden. It was spread tightly with a green mat
tatami. As one entered from the dusty ordinary classroom with its shuffling of feet, there was still calmness here. We all took off our shoes and quietly sat
with our knees together on the cold mat. The teacher,
who sat precisely in the center of the room, placed
both hands on the mat, quietly bent the upper half
of her body, lowered her head almost to the backs
of her hands, and gradually raised it again; once more
she bowed in the same manner, at the same time extending words of greeting: "It is very nice of you to
have come to this terribly shabby place. Are the members of your respected family all well?"

One by one we went before the teacher and performed the act of receiving a guest, feeling that we
had come from maidenhood to mistress' status. The
pupil next to me raised her right hand.

"Teacher, what does one do when receiving the
guest of an elder brother during his absence?"

As I waited for the teacher's answer, I was thinking that it must be very improper to receive a young man, even if he is a brother's friend.

The teacher, straightening the wrinkles from between her eyebrows, answered, "In a good home, they would never expect a young girl to do such a thing."

We who had been taught that social intercourse with young men was immoral, agreed with the teacher, without entertaining any doubt. It seemed to me that the world's young men were living in a barred castle which could only occasionally be glimpsed on its mist-shrouded mountaintop. Even to gaze toward the castle in our girlhood was to contaminate both mind and body, such a terrible thing it was.

Home Training

ELDER SISTER and I were walking along the main street. Women, children and peddlers, going in all directions, bustled around us. We turned into a side street, and everything was suddenly silent. Branches of purple magnolia drooped over the high black wooden fences which lined the curving lane. Dream-like, their fragrance floated through the spring air. There was not even a shadow of a passer-by. Our geta made far-away echoes as we sauntered leisurely past fences, trees and houses that dozed in the warm spring sun.

Following the curving lane, Elder Sister and I came to the gate of the temple. Two small sparrows were poised on its gray-tiled roof. We had arrived. We paused before the gate, took a deep breath, and composed ourselves. We had come for our first lesson in tea ceremony.

A few days before, Oba-san had said, "She who knows tea ceremony has, somehow, a manner of repose, a deep peace and culture. You two young ladies are now almost old enough to become brides, so I have arranged for lessons for you."

A path of steppingstones wound among trees to the temple. Quietly Nobu opened the outer shutter and called softly, "Pardon." From the cool stillness only the fragrant incense drifted to meet us. Then a small temple boy appeared, bowed silently, and led us beyond a long open veranda to the tea ceremony room. It was a small, four-and-a-half mat room, simple and austere. We knelt before the Tokonoma, our hands folded lightly on our knees.

Noiselessly the priest entered. He was tall like a sky-reaching tree. He wore a white garment, white obi, and even whiter *tabi* on his feet. His face was like smooth yellow ivory, his nose prominent, his forehead high. His shaved head looked pale green above the gleaming white vestment. I felt solemn majesty in his presence. He bowed in greeting and seated himself before us.

"The spirit of tea ceremony is the embodiment of the Zen philosophy," he said. "If only the form is learned, you have learned nothing." He drew his white hands up from his lap, clasped them gently, and closed his eyes. "Zen, as you know, is one sect of Buddhism. It comes from the Hindu word *Dhyan*, meaning 'peace, quiet, meditation in supreme repose.'" I watched the slow movement of his fingers like lotus petals, clasping and unclasping. He stood up glid-

87

ingly, almost without motion. "Now I will perform the ceremony. Please observe carefully." Bowing his head, he withdrew into the adjoining room.

First he brought in a bamboo basket filled with glossy cherry-wood charcoal, the end grain showing like petals of a flower; then two metal fire sticks, a purple-gray antique bowl, a bamboo whisk, and a small dipper. One by one he placed them on a low black-lacquered tray. We sat quietly, hardly drawing breath.

In one corner of the room an iron kettle with white steam gently rising, rested on the glowing coals of the *irori* hearth. The priest moved so soundlessly that even the air seemed still. I watched dazedly as he knelt before the hearth, his back toward the room.

Through the open end of the room I looked into the small temple garden. Thick brown pine needles matted the ground. A line of lichened rocks wound in and out, down to a stone lantern. I felt transported into some deep hidden forest, far from the dwelling of man. Elder Sister touched my knees with her fingertips, and I, startled, was brought back to the present world.

The priest, using a small spoon, was dipping the blue-green tea from a black-lacquered canister and putting it into the bowl. He picked up the little wooden dipper, placing the tips of his fingers evenly along the stem, and laid it horizontally across his hands before dipping it into the kettle. Slowly he poured hot water into the bowl, and returned the dipper to a corner of the tray. Then he picked up the whisk in the same manner, and gently stirred the mixture to a feathery foam.

"Tea ceremony is an art," he said in a low, clear voice as he placed the bowl before Nobu. He explained that in performing tea ceremony it is most essential to keep the graceful upper curve of the hand, with the fingers even at the tips.

I looked at the bowl Elder Sister was lifting. The foam had settled, and there was hardly more than a few teaspoonfuls of tea in the bottom. She daintily sipped three times, cupping the bowl in her hands and lifting it for each sip. Then she took a small folded paper napkin out of the bosom of her kimono, wiped the edge of the bowl lightly once, and passed the bowl to me. The thick green tea was bitter to my tongue, but the lingering after-taste was indescribably sweet.

The first lesson was over. As we walked out of the gate, I asked Elder Sister if she had understood about the Zen philosophy. She tilted her head to one side and said thoughtfully, "Supreme repose—supreme repose. In that quiet room I felt I understood, but now, in this helter-skelter, I really don't know."

About this time we also started lessons in flower arrangement. Our teacher was a woman about forty years old, dressed in severe dark kimono, with an overgarment of even darker hue. Her hair was cut short. When I was presented to her for the first time, I thought, "Ah, she is a *bibōjin*." This means "widow," or literally, "not yet dead person." It is the custom for a woman to cut her hair when her husband dies, and place it in his coffin before cremation. This shear-

89

ing of her most precious possession is a symbol that she is existing only physically, that her thoughts are always with the husband. I felt that this woman's personality was like a deep-rooted tree in dark forest, never touched by the rays of the sun. Looking at her earthen-image face, I wondered if it had ever known even a fleeting smile.

The teacher had brought with her a bundle of *nanten* branches and a silken bag containing her knives and red-handled shears. These she placed on the green grass mat, and, having bowed to us, she slipped silently down on her knees before them. She untied the green boughs, carefully took out the knives and shears, and began to trim the branches and bend them to shape. Elder Sister and I, wordless, watched the gentle motion of her fingers. In the stillness of the room the shears made a *pachin-pachin* sound. The teacher tilted her head a little and studied the bronze vase. She put in one branch, and sat back to look at the effect. Then she put in a second and a third, until there were about nine branches of different heights arranged in the vase.

Moving backward from the mat in one unbroken motion, she explained briefly and simply the spirit of flower arrangement. "It is the re-creation of the universe," she said. "The symbol of heaven, earth, and man, and expressing their unity."

The tallest branches symbolized heaven, the next man, the lowest earth. The teacher turned to Nobu and said, "Now, if you will, please arrange the flowers with this in mind."

90

Elder Sister slipped gracefully onto the mat, studied the arrangement with a solemn expression, carefully removed the branches one by one, and arranged them in the vase again. The teacher sat behind her, silently watching the way she used her hands. "It was well done, for the first time," she commended.

Then came my turn. Hopefully praying that I would be able to acquit myself as well as Elder Sister had, I removed the boughs one by one and laid them in order on the mat so that I would be able to remember their positions. Then I placed in the vase the tallest branch symbolizing heaven, and after it the others. As I finished and withdrew from the mat bowing, there was a loud swish. I lifted my head to find the vase turned over and the branches scattered like trees after a hurricane. Involuntarily I trembled, clasped my shoulders with crossed arms, and looked at the teacher out of the corner of my eyes. Without any expression on her face she slipped back onto the mat, took up the fallen boughs, and replaced them one by one.

I was determined to repair my disgrace, so I applied myself sedulously during flower arrangement lessons. As the lessons went on, we were allowed to trim and shape the branches ourselves. One day, when Elder Sister had left the room to get some water for the vase, the teacher said to me, "You are more gifted than your sister in flower arrangement and in the use of your hands."

I was speechless with surprise. I had always thought that Elder Sister far excelled me in everything. I

91

wanted to tell her what the teacher had said, but fearing to hurt her pride, I kept this secret to myself.

We were always happy when Saturday came, for we had school only half a day. But now we felt sadness too. Other girls returned home to play, but now we went to take lessons in penmanship. This was considered important training for brides, for one of the duties of a wife is to send beautifully written greetings to her husband's relatives.

Our penmanship teacher received us in a room facing her garden, the sliding doors opening onto the veranda. She sat with her back to the garden, kneeling before a low desk, and the pupils sat facing her. As I pushed the oblong inkstick on the flat black stone, I looked beyond the teacher to where intertwined branches of trees cast a lacy pattern on the reddish garden walks. In the room there was only the soothing sound of scraping inksticks; and I sat quietly, breathing the fragrance of ink and watching the changing shadows in the garden. As if in a dream I heard the teacher explain that inferior ink was gritty and did not run smoothly from the brush; that superior ink had delightful odor and followed the will of the brush, leaving a clear glossy stroke.

At first I did not understand that she was teaching us to transform the printed characters into cursive writing, so I made curves and flourishes at random. Without leaving her place the teacher would reach over and correct my writing. I marveled that she could correct it upside down when it was so difficult for me to write with the paper right side up.

92

My world in these days was a quiet world, like the mirrored surface of an ancient pool; without motion, without flow, reflecting the clear blue sky or the moving clouds, itself unchanged. Sometimes a wind ruffled the surface to waves, but it returned again to ancient, untroubled calm.

The Narikin and the Rice Riot

IN THE SUMMER of 1918, Elder Sister and I were invited to visit the family of our uncle at Lake Chuzenji in Nikko. This uncle, according to lineage, was far removed from us; but according to genealogy, our house was a branch which had separated from Uncle's several generations ago; Uncle's family was the main branch, and therefore its members were our closest relatives. Uncle had inherited through many generations an extensive wholesale clothing business. Besides this, he had acquired interests in some thirty factories which, during the World War, had shot up like bamboo shoots after rain. Riding on wartime prosperity, Uncle had started to live more opulently than we, and had recently bought a summer villa in Nikko. He was, in fact, one of the *"narikin,"* or newly rich, so severely criticized by the public, but I did

94

not know this. *"Narikin"* is a chess term for the chess-man who enters the enemy lines and becomes a gold general. I had kept a pure, small-girl antagonism to-ward these newly rich who spent money like water: once I had heard how a *narikin* in Osaka reveled, gaz-ing at the white skin of a geisha as she danced and frolicked in a room which he had filled full of golden-colored sake. I did not dream that my own uncle could be one of these people.

Nikko is surrounded by beautiful mountains and water, and at the foot of the mountains stands Toshogu, the mausoleum of Tokugawa Ieyasu, which has a collection of the finest pieces of art. Once I had been taken sight-seeing in Nikko by my second mother. Standing before the gold-and-silver-sculp-tured Yomei Gate at the entrance of Toshogu, Mother had said that it was called Day-waning Gate because one can gaze at it all day and still its beauties are not exhausted when day draws to a close.

Holding to my heart the half-burnt remembrance of that visit to Nikko with Mother, I got off the train. The base of the mountain ranges stretched to our feet, and the mountain spirit, echoing the water-sound in the gorges, wrapped me gently in itself. Elder Sister and I rocked up the slowly rising moun-tain path in the jinrikisha which had been sent to meet us, and watched the water of the gorge at our feet. The water was blue and so clear that it seemed that one could pick up the small stones lying deep at the bottom of the gorge. The rapid waters broke whitely between sharp granite crags and scattered like flower petals. The narrow suspension bridge across the gorge moved swayingly as the kuruma went over it. I remembered suddenly how, as we approached the bridge, Mother had said it was cold and had put a *furoshiki* over the head of timid me.

Gradually we looked down on the peaks of the mountain range, and at last we came to the shores of Chuzenji Lake at the top of the range. Chuzenji Lake, quietly reflecting densely luxuriant Cryptomeria, was blue and clear. Uncle's villa on the opposite side of the lake stood as though embraced by the mountain side and the tall Cryptomeria.

The villa was built in both Western and Japanese style, and had countless rooms. Beyond the full-blooming rose garden was a billiard room; on the opposite side was a garden with a rustic gate; behind the stone lantern and the pine branches, the white shoji of the elaborate tea room was visible.

That night, for the first time, I slept on a Western bed instead of on a quilt spread over a mat. I lay on my back on the bed, happy at the softness and the feeling that my body floated in space, as though I were riding on clouds through the sky. Elder Sister peered at my face. "Haru, be careful not to fall off the bed, *ne*," she said solemnly.

The next morning I awoke and looked quickly around me. My body was still on the bed, but the silken feather comforter had slipped to the floor. Stepping stealthily, I picked it up and went over to the window. Against the dawning sky the faraway mountain ranges piled up in faint purplish lines through floating morning mist. Gradually, as if heavenly bodies danced down and unfolded transparent garments, light spread over the ranges. At Uncle's villa even the natural scenery seemed to reach the limit of extravagance.

After breakfast we were taken by Aunt for a walk to Kegon Falls. Young and beautiful Aunt had wrapped her slender body in a kimono of soft silk crepe, demure, with a light blue background. We were wearing ordinary kimonos of coarse silk, and when we stood before Aunt's lithe silken form we felt stiffly starched, as if we would make a *gowa-gowa* noise. When we went trout fishing in the afternoon, Aunt changed to a gauze crepe kimono of blue background with a design of bamboo leaves.

There were a number of Occidental people at the trout hatchery. The Occidental women walked with their chests thrust out and seemed actually to be tipping backward. One of them who stood with a fishing rod near me incessantly said something to me, but I could not understand her and so I looked blankly at her face. As I looked, I thought I saw whiskers growing at the corners of her mouth. Later, when I asked Uncle about this, he said, "American women imitate everything men do, so there are many women who even put on mustaches like men." Since men with mustaches are usually university professors or higher officials, I wondered if women in America put on mustaches when they became accomplished.

Supper, unlike the noonday meal, was in pure Occidental style. I worried lest I misuse the many differ-

97

ent-shaped knives and forks arranged on the table. Thinking how calamitous that would be, I hid behind Elder Sister and glanced sideways at Aunt's way of handling them. Perhaps because of my worry, the Occidental meal which I usually liked so much seemed to stick in my chest.

That night the lake, sinking into evening darkness, was like a dream world. The evening primrose suddenly unfolded its lovely bloom. I loved this flower which in the evening dusk by the side of the lake opened its flower bashfully and all alone gazed up at the moon.

One evening early in August, Uncle, Aunt, Elder Sister and I went out for a walk along the lake shore in the direction of the souvenir shops which sold picture postcards and handicraft work. The lake reflected the lights of lanterns, and on the shore a water fowl spread and flapped its white wings. All at once the sound of bells and the cry of "Extra! Extra!" pierced the peaceful stillness. A newspaper boy came dashing toward us, his head-band knotted in front, the bells on his hips sounding *jaran-jaran*. Uncle bought a paper and glanced at it, and the color of his face changed. He began to walk, in silence, with hurrying feet. Almost running after him, we returned home.

The extra reported that a riot had begun as a protest against the doubling of the price of rice. It said that from moment to moment the riot was spreading. Fishermen's wives in a fishing village in Toyama Prefecture had raised a clamor. Eventually this riot

98

spread to the great cities of Kyoto, Osaka and Kobe, and led finally to the mobilization of the army.

Uncle, agitated, decided to leave at once for Tokyo. Elder Sister and I, sitting on either side of Aunt, strained after the sound of Uncle's limousine as it faded into the quiet darkness. Aunt said that she would be lonesome by herself, and so we slept that night in the room next to her bedroom. I lay in bed and saw in my mind a glistening white mountain of rice and the forms of fishermen's wives who could not buy it. As I closed my eyes, the memory of a beggar woman and her child whom I had seen in the street came to me fleetingly and it seemed to me that they were saying something. . . .

The next morning Aunt carefully read the paper which she generally only glanced at after Uncle had finished reading it. Under a headline, KOBE'S RICE RIOT, there was a short article reporting that a mob of twenty thousand had advanced on Suzuki Firm, which was reputed to have raised the price of rice by buying it up, and had attacked the rice warehouses.

"Isn't it terrible that ignorant people act like this?" Aunt said to Elder Sister, lifting her eyes from the newspaper. "Of course, I feel sorry for people who can't buy rice because the price is so high, but wouldn't it be better if they would request things quietly? Isn't it outrageous of them to throw stones and kick through the doors of Suzuki Firm's rice warehouses?"

Elder Sister agreed vigorously, and looked at the paper. "Oh honorable Aunt," she said, "it says here that the soldiers folded their arms and let the mob do as they pleased. It says, 'Soldiers seem in their inner minds to sympathize with the crowd.'"

Aunt said, "Because of such things the riot is spreading. In our house we always contribute to charity and are kind to the people, but still an increasing number of them return evil for good." She sighed, worried perhaps about Uncle's business affairs.

Late that night Uncle returned from Tokyo; but he continued to go busily back and forth. The rice riot, which had begun early in August, continued for over a month, and spread through most of the nation, disturbingly. At the same time, strikes sprang up here and there. Uncle, who usually talked only about trout fishing or motorboating, now talked ill-temperedly about the rice riot and the strikes.

"In Japan," he said, "there is a beautiful custom of parent and son relationship, and workers and employers have lived harmoniously like one family. To express it in a broader sense, the entire Japanese nation is one peaceful family—helping each other in times of trouble, worrying for each other. But the workers nowadays have twisted minds and don't consider masters as masters. This is the bad influence of foreign materialistic civilization."

I could only look dazedly at the dizzily flowing torrent of society. I had the faintly ominous feeling one has on a clear summer day when in a corner of the sky the rain clouds boil up suddenly and everything is dark. But, as when the rain is over, the feeling faded away.

100

Two autumns after this, Uncle, hurled into the storm of the post-War depression, was forced to surrender to other hands the Nikko villa and the big store handed down to him through generations; the furniture which he had also inherited from past generations was hauled desolately into our storeroom. Because of his inability to pay the debts of the thirty factories for which he was responsible, he became a marked man of the bill collectors and had to go into hiding. In his extravagant residence in Tokyo, with its heavy doored gate, emptiness and silence were settling. I visited Aunt in her small hiding-out house with its wicket door. She still retained her rich young mistress' elegance, and wore a heavy crepe haori serenely on her shoulders. But as I sipped the tea brought out by Aunt's own hands, I noticed that on the beautiful *Imari*-ware teacup before her, the gold-flower design on red background was cracked off, like chipped teeth. I was startled, as if I had seen something which I should not have seen, and silently I drooped my head.

1919

I WAS HURRYING home in the rain. Night was coming on, and I was caught up in a dense crowd returning from work. Although I was carrying an armful of books and holding my paper umbrella high and lifting my skirt to protect it from mud, still I walked as if in a dream. Only when I was jostled by someone was I aware of those about me. My thoughts were still at the Y.W.C.A., whence I had come.

The soft thin rain, clearing my thoughts, stirred in me feelings impossible to communicate. I was living in a world of my own, a world of radiance and promise, and in the center of this world was myself. I knew that there was something inside me that did not belong to my house, that did not belong to my country, that was neither my family's nor my ancestors', but was all mine. For some time now I had caught these hitherto undiscovered truths in snatches of poetry

102

which floated through my mind. And tonight the deep resonance of the hymn which had been sung at the "Y" before the meeting ended re-echoed inside me and found a response. I had not dared to sing it with the others—I was unable to keep a tune. But as I turned into our quiet street I slowed down and murmured, "The Lord is my shepherd. I shall not want. He maketh me to lie down in green pastures. He restoreth my soul. . . ." And suddenly I knew that the queer fluttering inside me was my own soul. The hushed stillness, the sweet scent of air, agreed that it was so.

After school that afternoon I had gone to the library for an English textbook. Instead of returning home, I had found myself at the "Y." A woman I had never seen was speaking from the platform. Her talk was about a labor conference that was to be held in Washington, the capital of her country. She said that it had grown out of the Versailles Treaty, and that it offered the people of Japan a great opportunity to discuss their aims, their needs, and their difficulties with representatives of other countries. When she said that it would help to make a lasting peace for the entire world and to end the increasing number of strikes throughout Japan, I felt happy. She told of a large meeting to be held that night by Yuai Kai, the Friendly Laborers' Society. A Japanese Christian lawyer had started the society to educate workers, and he was still the head of it. I could not follow all that she said, but I felt drawn into a larger world. After some more speeches and prayers, a woman in a long black dress with a little lace collar played the piano. I was shy and slipped out of the meeting, my head in the clouds.

When I arrived at the side entrance of our house, I still felt warm and soft and pure inside, but not quite so secure in the possession of my own soul. I slipped out of my high clogs, washed, changed my clothes, and entered the dining room. Elder Sister, Younger Brother and Oba-san were already seated on their cushions. Father was not at home. I gave the customary greeting, but it was met with icy stares. We ate our food in silence. I picked at mine. I knew I was in disgrace. My world had narrowed, and I was unable to recapture my former mood.

Just before dinner ended, Nobu spoke, her voice sounding far away. "Why did not my sister attend tea-ceremony lesson today?"

So that was it. Again I had neglected my womanly duties. I explained that I had gone to the library for an English textbook and had stopped at the "Y" for only a second, but that there had been such a wonderful meeting that I had stayed. I told her it was important for me to improve my English by hearing it spoken properly.

My brother said contemptuously, "It is ridiculous for a girl to study English as seriously as a boy does." I had invaded his masculine world and hurt his pride.

Elder Sister, conscious of the fact that she was shortly to graduate from high school, was very superior: "You listen to these foreigners too seriously. They have a bad influence on us. We must learn to take

104

what we want from them without becoming like them. My morals teacher warned us about the women especially. She said that in America they have a rapidly developed civilization, without culture, without standards; they have had to build up their morals because they aren't born with them as we are. She said that we wouldn't have a labor problem here if it weren't for the Americans and other foreigners who want the Japanese women to hate the men and make them restless."

I wanted to tell Nobu she wasn't right. The woman at the "Y" had spoken not of hate but of love and righteousness. But I could find no words to express my thoughts; I did not know how to explain that I had not accepted what she said and that I wanted to be drawn into a wider world.

That night I did not sleep very well, and I awoke early in the morning. The sun was shining brightly when I went into the dining room and picked up the morning paper. It was full of *Rodo Mondai,* the labor problem. It told of the arrest of a Mr. Toyohiko Kagawa, who was one of the leaders in a strike of fifteen thousand workers in the Kawasaki Shipbuilding Yards in Kobe. The workers were striking for the unheard-of workday of eight hours. The newspaper story made fun of a member of the committee of strikers who, when he was asked for the meaning of collective bargaining, said, "I will reply tomorrow when I have consulted the committee."

There was an editorial in the paper which praised the action of Doctor Yoshino, a professor of Tokyo

Imperial University, and Mr. Kitazawa, a professor of Waseda University, in withdrawing from the Friendly Love Society because it had endorsed the Government's delegates to the Washington Peace Conference.

Then there was a long article about the meeting of the Yuai Kai. Here for the first time a woman worker had addressed an audience. She had spoken with a baby strapped to her back. She said that she and her husband together made less than sixty Yen a month— not enough to feed and care for her family properly. She said that she had to work such long hours that she had no time for her husband and children. She asked for shorter hours, and for one day of rest a week instead of the one day a month which the workers in her factory were given. Another speaker said that the workers wanted to send their own delegate to Washington and not accept the one chosen by the Government. He said that the Government delegate would only stress racial discrimination in other countries, and the workers wanted to push their own demands. Resolutions were passed asking for shorter hours, a higher rate of pay, and the right to organize. The chairman said that the unrest among the people was due, not to outside influence, but to the industrialization of Japan and to the increasing number of accidents in the factories. He said that if the Government would encourage the workers to organize, there would be better discipline among them and fewer riots.

All of this sounded very interesting, but it did not touch or affect my life in any way. I was glad that my

106

country was being represented in this extraordinary labor conference, but I did not understand most of the new words used in the newspaper, and since Father was not at home I could not find out what they meant.

After breakfast, while I was running about collecting our school things, Nobu said, "You see, it's just as I told you. Imagine a working-class woman with a baby on her back speaking before a large audience, telling her troubles. It is just as my teacher said. It is a disgrace to the women of Japan. The outside world will think that all Japanese women are like that. Why can't she keep her troubles to herself instead of being disrespectful to her employers? She should be grateful to them."

I admired Nobu for her ability to present her thoughts. I wished that I might express mine as well, but they were only a series of impressions, none of which I was able to define. Instead of trying, I said, "We must hurry. Today is the day my class has factory inspection and a visit to the slums."

I made no connection between what I had just read and this proposed trip. The one dealt with the outside world, the other was part of my school work. Because of the great interest in labor problems throughout Japan, these trips were arranged for high school and college students. We were not prepared for them. There was no discussion of them beforehand. We were not to have any opinions. We were not to analyze. We were not to draw any conclusions. We were merely to observe.

The teacher led the students along the Sen River. This river had once been a bay, but now it was a narrow open sewer in which garbage and refuse were thrown. Black oil floated on top of the water. When Tokyo had rain for three or more successive days, the river banks overflowed, and the foul refuse caused epidemics of typhus, typhoid fever, scarlet fever, and skin diseases, which often spread to other parts of the city. We tried to hold our breath so as not to take in that vile odor.

On both sides of the river were small shacks. They were built on the muddy banks without foundations, and they sank ever deeper into the earth. They were so low we could almost touch their roofs. Outside of them, torn kimonos and underwear hung over bamboo poles extending horizontally from the roofs. Our own soft purple and red *hakama* skirts were vivid in that drab neighborhood.

Little children with strained eyes and running noses stared at us with open mouths. When we looked at them, they ran away like so many little birds.

We turned into a narrow street where with outstretched arms we could touch the houses on both sides. The doors were broken and the paper screens were torn so that we could see inside. Out of these huts came, not the lusty cries of healthy babies, but the sorrowful wails of weak and sick babies. We stopped in front of one of the houses and peeked through the torn paper screen. The interior was dark and seemed unoccupied. Torn bedding lay on the

108

floor, with dirty gray cotton—once white—tumbling out of it.

Tingling with the drama of poverty, I thought to myself, "Such misery is but the way of the world."

Suddenly the bedding moved. Two eyes glared out at us. A voice shouted, "Get away from here. I am not an animal in a zoo!"

My poetic feelings thrown to the winds, my heart beating wildly, I ran with the other girls. One of them said, "How could he be so rude and frighten us?"

When the teacher, walking with measured pace, caught up with us, she said, "It is not good manners for well-bred young ladies to run in panic no matter how rudely they may be spoken to. These low creatures deserve their misery; it is of their own making. We have seen enough. Now we will proceed to the factory."

A half-hour's walk through narrow winding streets brought us in view of a high brick wall towering upward like a cliff. The houses around it seemed to be bowing low on the earth. Something shone and gleamed around the top of the wall. When we came nearer, I saw that it was a row of sharp, jagged pieces of glass which jutted out like so many swords. The purpose of them was to prevent anyone's escaping from inside or climbing over from the outside. Two guards, swinging their clubs, were posted on either side of the double iron gate of the factory. They opened the gate for us. A cold tremor went down my back as quietly we entered a bare, sinister courtyard.

This textile factory was built in Western style, but

inside the woodwork was unpainted and had turned black. We were met by company officials who bowed ceremoniously. One of them said, "We welcome the opportunity to show you our modern factory." He stepped forward and led us into a large room. The machinery was whirring with such a tremendous sound that I thought it would break my eardrums. A three-inch belt ran fast with wave-like motion, and out of it came groaning, angry sounds which reverberated from the walls, the ceiling, the windows. The clashing sounds seemed to bite and quarrel with each other. The company official stood in the center of the room, between rows of machines. I saw his mouth moving, but his voice vanished into the noise. Around the room were pipes out of which came a misty steam which made the fiber strong. The room was kept at a temperature of eighty-five degrees fahrenheit. In the moist air the machinery created a wind, and millions of tiny, feathery bits of cotton whirled and settled on the faces and shoulders of the girls.

Each girl was managing four of the fast-moving machines. I looked at the girl in front of me, met her glassy stare, and turned away. Directly in front of me in that colorless room was a piece of faded red cloth. I wondered what it meant until the official explained that it was a warning to the girls that badly woven cloth would not be tolerated. He told us that there were four grades of cloth. The first grade guaranteed the girl full wages—sixty sen a day, or fifteen cents in American money; second-grade cloth deducted 2 per cent from her wages; third-grade cloth cut the wages

110

in half; and fourth-grade cloth gave her no pay at all. He said that the wages were higher here than in most factories, and so they had to insist on good quality. It takes about two days to make a length of cloth of twenty-eight *shaku,* or nine yards. I later learned that when the cloth was bad it was usually due, not to the girls, but to the poor machines and the inferior cotton with which they worked.

The official pointed to a list of names on a large sheet of paper hung on the wall:

> *Koyama Ito—12 sen—third grade*
> *Mori Taki—no sen—fourth grade*
> (*etc.*)

Turning to us, he said, "All the girls are ashamed to make a bad grade. They all work very hard for the first grade and cry if their names appear on the paper."

We looked back at the girls. They were about the same age as we. Some were panting and limping. We did not know then that 20 per cent of these girls had beriberi; that their feet were so swollen that the least unevenness in the floor caused them to fall. We looked at them as though we were watching a play— and thought we were bringing a certain amount of gaiety and pleasure by our presence. Their lips were moving as they worked. I couldn't hear their words, but it was not long afterward that I heard of the songs which had been in vogue since Japan first had textile mills. They were songs composed by the girls them- selves, with words like these:

111

The factory is just like a hell,
Our foreman is like a devil,
The turning wheel is like a wheel of fire,
The work in the factory is like prison in a cell
Only without metal chains. . . .

The official, grinning broadly, led us into the dining room. It was a fair-sized room, with long, bare, unbroken rows of benches and tables.

"Most of these girls are from the country," he told us. "In their homes they eat only barley. Here we give them hot white rice, so they are better fed than they would be at home. They used to eat in shifts, but now we stop all of the machinery so that they can eat at the same time."

In answer to a question of the teacher he said that the factory law provided that the girls work only twelve hours a day, but that most of them took advantage of the privilege of working an hour overtime to earn an extra five sen—the equivalent of a cent and a half in American money. He took out his watch and looked at it. "It is about time for the girls' lunch," he said. "It is better for us to leave."

He led us to the door. As we were leaving the dining room we heard the signal for lunch. The girls were unable to hear the blast, and so a flag was waved inside the room as a signal. The lunch period was half an hour, and the girls had to clean their machines before they could eat. They didn't stop to wash their hands, for there was little enough time left. The suddenly quiet halls resounded to waves of running steps.

The dining room was in turmoil, and I could hear some of the conversation. The dining room attendant was saying, "All these girls are pigs."

"We don't mind if we are pigs or horses, just give us our food," the girls shouted back.

I blushed at this conversation.

We left the noise behind us and went on to the dormitories. The rooms here were in Japanese style, with mat floors, and they all had elegant names: Pine Tree Room, Plum Blossom Room, Bamboo Room. The official said that 80 per cent of mill workers were girls; that in some mills only half of the girls slept in, but that it was their policy to have all the girls sleep in dormitories. There were two hundred girls in this factory, and two girls shared one quilt.

"The parents of these girls have entrusted them to us," he said. "We have accepted this grave responsibility, and we watch carefully over their daily lives. We think it unwise for such young girls to go out more than once a month. Once a month two or three girls are permitted to leave together, but they must return before ten o'clock in the evening. That is an inflexible rule."

He showed us a magazine called *Koshu No Haha* (*The Mother of the Weaver*), which the factory published for the girls. At the bottom of the cover was inscribed:

WORK HARD WITHOUT COMPLAINT

IT IS FOR YOUR COUNTRY. FOR YOUR PARENTS.

FOR YOUR HAPPINESS.

He said, "We feel we can best safeguard our girls from dangerous and corrupting thoughts by publishing our own paper instead of letting them read papers and magazines from outside."

With many bows he led us to the door. He told us that he hoped we had a better understanding of the way a modern factory was run, and of the humane considerations which prompted the company to protect the girls. The teacher, with many apologies for having kept him from his lunch, assured him that the young girls in her charge quite appreciated the work being accomplished here.

I had held back, and now I caught up with the others with a troubled heart. When the girls returned to their machines, before the noise started up, I had heard them singing in low, sad voices:

Each spring the cherry buds open,
Each spring cherry blossoms fall,
But they will bloom again next spring.
The flowers in my heart never open.
When will my flowers bloom?

I am only a slave girl,
A little bird
Who cannot fly, even if I had wings;
I can see the sky, but I am in a cage;
I am a little, little bird
Without wings. . . .

Elder Sister's Wedding

ELDER SISTER NOBU was sewing, oblivious to her surroundings. The red silk lining spread over her lap fell in bright folds under the electric light. The sound of silken thread drawn through her fingers flowed softly into the autumn evening. Elder Sister was voiceless, as though her mind and spirit were engrossed. Her *momoware* haircomb with the red tied and dyed hair-cloth leaned a little heavily to one side.

To sew well was considered one of woman's chief accomplishments. As a child, tirelessly I had watched my mother's hands as she sewed my clothes. Then I had prayed that I would soon be able to do sewing. But now my mind was filled with thoughts so stormy and agitating that to sew quietly was wearisome. When my clothes became soiled, I ripped the seams

115

and sent them to be washed and dried on boards. These pieces had again to be sewn together, and this much I did, sewing up my own ordinary kimono with my own hands. But now I sat by the *hibachi,* running my eyes over the papers, aimlessly.

To me, Elder Sister with the *Nihon* haircomb, absorbedly moving her hands, was like a woman in a picture book of a long, long time ago. Elder Sister had been a sympathetic, comforting mother to motherless me. But that mother-image living in my mind was effaced now, sucked away into darkness. Elder Sister no longer even tried to peer into my thoughts. Even though we sat in the same room, we were far apart. We were living in different mental worlds.

The kettle on the *hibachi* began to boil, making a *chin-chin* sound. The steam coming out of the spout cast a swaying shadow on the wall. As I rustled the papers in my hands, Elder Sister said in a very quiet voice:

"Haru, although I haven't told you until now, matters have finally progressed to *Omiai.*" Flushing slightly, Elder Sister put her sewing to one side.

"*Omiai?*" I repeated the word, echoingly. *Miai* is the formal meeting, face to face, of the prospective parties to a marriage. Before this, the go-between exchanges the photographs of the two parties. I remembered Elder Sister's worrying about her pictures, going back repeatedly to be rephotographed when they did not meet with her approval.

"This person, I think, is my ideal. For, first of all, he is a graduate of Imperial University, does not drink

116

sake, and his interests are many." Since a graduate of Imperial University has a promise for the future, Elder Sister considered this a first requirement.

I lowered the newspaper to my knees and steadily looked at Elder Sister's face. Her mind, deciding on marriage merely by looking at a photograph, seemed strange and not to be measured.

"But aren't you worried about deciding on a husband whom you do not know very well?"

"Well, besides the photograph, a complete investigation has been made of his school records, his interests, his family's affairs, his family tree. Haru, everyone marries in this way."

Japanese marriage binds family to family, and there is no consideration given to mutual love.

"But, Elder Sister, can you like a person just by seeing one photograph and then having the *Omiai?* Can you love him? In Ellen Kay's book it says that to marry without love is immoral."

About this time a new way of thinking and new words were becoming fashionable. Words like *ren ai*, "love between a man and a woman." I did not know the mystery and beauty of love, but I felt drawn toward the word.

"You mustn't use such a wanton word as *ren ai*, Haru. Although you like to use new words, *ren ai* really means dalliance between a man and a woman. A fine marriage and *ren ai* are altogether different things. Be careful when you talk about these things."

"But, but—" I was a little angry. "To marry like you, isn't it like being a prostitute in Yoshiwara? In

117

the last analysis, I think it is the same thing as selling your own body."

"Haru, such horrid things—" Elder Sister began, and then bent over her work. Her gently sloping shoulders shook a little. I listened to her sobbing, dazed. I had had no intention of making her cry.

Elder Sister raised her face wet with tears, and said, "When you were small, Grandmother used to say what a good bride you would be. The Haru who used always to imitate me so docilely, why has she changed so much?"

As though to look deeply into me, Elder Sister put her hands on my knees. I grasped her hands gently, thinking that I had said inexcusable things.

The next day, while Elder Sister was absent at the hairdresser's, the maid told me a secret. She said that my sister's fiancé's mother was stopping casually in the neighborhood, at the rice dealer's, at the wine shop where we traded, to investigate my sister's reputation. "Anyway, the fiancé's mother finds your elder sister to her liking," the maid added with a serious expression. It was easy at this time to credit anything even slightly disadvantageous to Elder Sister, to me, the younger sister.

After the *miai* was concluded, the talk progressed rapidly. Betrothal presents were exchanged, and a lucky day at the end of December was selected for the marriage ceremony.

I looked at two-year-older Elder Sister gazing at the dyed marriage ceremony kimono, and felt a coldness in my heart. Was the same fate waiting for me

118

two years hence? Since childhood I had been taught
that to marry when one became of age was a woman's
way and a duty toward one's parents. But the thought
of marriage was like a mountain towering hazily in
the distance beyond the plain, and though I approached it and approached it, still it was eternally
far away. Now, looking at Elder Sister going as bride,
I felt the mountain close before me.

The day of Elder Sister's wedding was a cold, clear
winter day. The afternoon sun, slanting obliquely,
dropped pale light on the veranda of the living room.
The time was nearing for us to go together to the marriage ceremony, which was to be performed at Hibiya
Daijingu, the great shrine.

Since morning the hairdresser and kimono dresser
had beseiged our house, and Elder Sister, hiding behind a screen in a large room removed from the household, had not once shown her face. I, wearing a
suso-moyo kimono with a hem-design and with obi
tied high on my breast, waited for Elder Sister to
finish her preparations. I had felt no spirit to wear a
new kimono and to adorn myself; my mind, filled
with more important questions, was impatient with
such things. But when I had said that I would not care
if I wore a Western dress which I happened to have,
Grandmother had said it was unseemly, and had sent
a *suso-moyo* kimono.

The noisy wheel-sound of the kuruma, which was
taking out Elder Sister's luggage, stopped suddenly,
and everything was quiet. The pine tree, with the
yellow straw cap to protect it against snow, stood

119

solemnly in the garden. Father came downstairs and entered the room in which I sat. He was wearing striped trousers and a cutaway.

"Do you think Nobu will be ready soon? When she is, please come with her to the reception room." So saying, he left the room.

Soon there was a sound of quiet footsteps and silken rustle, and the flower-bride shape of Elder Sister appeared before me. To me she was more like a beautifully dressed doll than like a living person. We opened the shoji of the reception room where Father and Younger Brother were waiting, holding their hands over the *hibachi*. Younger Brother, wearing his closely-buttoned school uniform, sat on a cushion uncomfortably. Entering behind Elder Sister, I sat beside Younger Brother.

Father said, "This is the final time that the three of you and Father will sit here as one family, *ne*. So thinking, I asked you all to meet here. Nobu, for a long time you have taken care of Younger Brother and Younger Sister. You have also devoted yourself well to Father. I want to thank you for all these things. I am happy for you too, Nobu, that the match is so good. But when Father thinks that you are leaving this house forever, various thoughts come floating to his mind." As though suddenly overwhelmed, Father cut short his words. Was he thinking, if only Mother were alive? Then he continued in a more formal tone:

"Nobu, until now this has been your home. From now on your home is that to which you go as bride.

Besides that there is no other. I suppose you understand."

Elder Sister, who had been sitting silently with head bowed, quietly raised her face. "Father, I understand your words well. I thank you for having cared for me until now." A tear fell, spattering, on the back of her hands folded in her lap. Was her heart stung by the sorrow of eternal separation from herself as daughter?

"So, if we don't leave, we shall be late," Father said, and got up; but Elder Sister only drooped her head. When she raised it finally, the face with the make-up was wet with tears.

The kimono dresser, flustered, took Elder Sister into the powder room, saying, "Please don't cry any more, *ne*," and touched up her face.

"I always have a hard time," she complained. "There are so many flower-brides who cry just before leaving."

When we arrived at Hibiya Daijingu, the world was dusking grayly, and the great torii was thrown like a silhouette against the purple-colored sky. The Shinto priest, with headgear and flowing robe reminiscent of many-centuried ancient time, came out and led us to the main shrine. The bride and bridegroom knelt before the shrine. Elder Sister was dressed in a long-sleeved *suso-moyo* kimono of black background, dyed with green pine and a large silver crane flying; the bridegroom wore Western swallowtail.

Quietly the Shinto priest approached them, holding in his hands the *gohei*, symbol of sanctity. He began

121

to wave it above the bride and groom, from left to right, mumbling, chanting, repeating, "Shake off evil! Purify!" The long black tail-like decoration of his headgear swung back and forth above the priest's head. Closing his eyes, he kept on waving the *gohei*. I trembled lest its white paper fringes get tangled in Elder Sister's high *Shimada* haircomb. But Elder Sister did not move one line of her forehead, and the groom kneeling beside her made not even one slight motion.

When the priest had completed the rites of purification, the bride and bridegroom, taking one by one the three red-lacquered wine cups piled up on the unpainted wooden tray, poured for each other and pledged troth one to the other. To me it seemed that such formality did not really bind two minds together, and I knew a great uneasiness.

After the ceremony of marriage-before-gods was over, we went to the marriage-announcing banquet, to which great numbers of relatives and friends had been invited. Elder Sister, changing from ceremonial kimono of black background with green pine, put on a *suso-moyo* kimono of light green background with gay design of a large flower of peach color, yellow, and purple. As senior to Father, the professor of the Imperial University who had been formal go-between, introduced the flower-bride and groom to everyone, felicitated the happy troth between the two families, and drank a toast.

Covertly I studied Elder Sister. She sat calm, serenely dignified, without a trace of perturbation. Her eyes pleasantly greeted the gaze of the many guests. Had she no anxiety for the life into which she was going? Until yesterday a stranger, today a husband attended by her as wife. . . . Could she thus surrender her own mind without misgiving?

When the banquet was over, I hid behind a hemp palm tree in the corner of the room so that I would not be seen. And again I wondered if the fate of Elder Sister was the only path open to me. To my mind suddenly came the words which Oba-san had dropped once long ago: "The first year, from dawn to dusk each day I thought continuously, 'Shall I return home today? Tomorrow resolutely I will leave my husband's house!' But after the first year a child arrived, and I completely put away such thoughts. When you are young, you may think this or that, but the world does not go the way you would like. . . ."

The gay laughing voices receded far away as I sat lost in thought. From behind me someone tapped my shoulder.

"My, hiding in such a place!"

I turned and saw that it was the woman who was the real go-between for my sister—a widow of about fifty years, who acted in this capacity, partly for her own amusement.

"The next time it will be yours, *ne*," she said matter-of-factly. "Be sure to give me your photograph, please. I will find you a fine family."

The woman withdrew, as though swimming through the reception room. I glanced around. Father and Elder Sister were happily surrounded by guests.

123

The guests were all carefree and gay. I alone stayed with heavy heart behind the potted hemp palm. I felt as though my body were bound by many layers of unseen threads, and I wondered how I could cut the threads and fly away to my own domain. I stood at the window and looked at the winter sky. The small stars glittered there like small sparks falling. And in my heart the poet's words were falling:

> *Somewhere*
> *To escape,*
> *But unable to flee,*
> *With heavy heart*
> *I gaze at the wide sky.*
> —Yosano Akiko

PART THREE

Jiyu Gakuen

MY FIVE YEARS of high school were over, and I felt my happy girlhood days flying from under my feet. The farewell words sung to us by the underclass girls rang sorrowfully in my ears:

> *Light of fireflies . . .*
> *Snow by the window . . .*
> *Days and months of study fly.*
> *Ere I'm aware the year has ended,*
> *Comes the day when I must hie.*

At the close of graduation day my friends and I wept under a Paulownia tree in the schoolyard. The principal had said to us in parting, "I felicitate your future as good wives and wise mothers." My friends, leaving me, were to be married soon, according to their parents' plans. My mind and body were bound with fear of a like destiny.

Father, sympathetic to my wishes, gave me permission to attend Jiyu Gakuen. This school, in which new educational methods were practiced, had been founded by Motoko Hani, the leader of the women of our country. Even the name, Jiyu Gakuen, gripped and bewitched my mind vaguely yearning for freedom. The school was in Musashi-no Plain in the suburbs of Tokyo. It was surrounded by tall oak trees bearing the marks of age; and the building, the work of the American architect, Mr. Wright, rested on the ground like a living, breathing thing—like a bird with its two wings spreading low.

Whenever I walked along the narrow path through the luxuriant grove and looked at the school building whitely shining in the morning sun, I thought of Madame Motoko Hani's talk to the assembled pupils on the day I entered Jiyu Gakuen. Thirty years ago this woman had begun to fight against the unreasonable restrictions on women in a men's world. She told us about her experiences: "When I was first hired as proofreader on a magazine," she said, "everyone would come and peer in my face, remarking that a woman had come in and how rare it was. The proofreading room in which I worked had a wire screen on the window, and people passing to and fro whispered audibly, 'A woman has come to the zoo!' " Her talk remained in my mind, ever encouraging me.

Madame Hani maintained that education could not be found in the classroom alone, that it was necessary to dip into real society. In order to give us this direct contact with society, she sometimes let the students give concerts and plays in first-class theaters. At other times she sent us to interview well-known people or to observe social work, and let us publish our impressions in a long-established ladies' magazine, *The Lady's Friend.*

I, who was a student of literature, was sent to interview Mr. Vorhis, an American who lived by Lake Biwa in Ohmi, and to observe the social work he was doing. The trip to Ohmi took one full day by train; I had never traveled so long a distance by myself. I spent a night at Mr. Vorhis' home, visited his nursery and Sunday School, and saw his tuberculosis sanitarium on the lake a few miles away. The white-gowned figures of the patients standing motionless by the sun-lit glass windows of the sanitarium, and the yellow blossoms of the globe flowers blooming wildly on the hillside, remained in the depths of my eyes. I could not forget these people who gazed at the clear blue lake and the wild flowers under the window, day after day, and each day with but one desire—good health. I wrote an article on what I had seen and received payment for it from *The Lady's Friend.* This was the first bit of money I had ever earned.

My trip had brought me close to people forgotten by society, and I felt that it had opened wide my eyes which until now had been closed.

One day, on the way home from school, I stopped at a friend's house. I did not want to spend the long spring Saturday afternoon alone, and in my own home there was no one to share my thoughts. I wanted to talk to this friend who was interested in the various

129

social questions which all at once were knocking against each other in my mind. She lived with her brother in a temple near our home, and she attended Jiyu Gakuen.

The temple yard, so thickly grown with tall Gingko trees that it was dark even in daytime, was delightful, cooling my seething mind. One of the temple rooms, incense-filled, was still as a deep forest. I sat with my friend, and after a while from the main hall of the temple a bell song floated out, dragging its long after-sound. A low voice chanting the sutra drifted into the evening dusk, and I stared into the garden trees that were wrapped in a green mist. When I parted from my friend, we had arranged to go the next day to the seashore, where we sometimes went after school to sketch.

As I walked around the high temple wall and passed the police box on the street corner, I heard a policeman's voice behind me rebuking someone. I was already late returning home, and so I walked with hurrying steps, not looking back. Then his voice called close to my ears: "Hey there! That short-sleeved dress! Your arms are sticking out!"

I looked involuntarily down at my arms. They were exposed, but it was a Western dress I was wearing, and I couldn't help it.

"Make those sleeves longer so that you won't corrupt public morals!" the policeman said.

Recently I had begun wearing Western dress, and a few days before, I had cut off my long flowing hair. At Jiyu Gakuen pupils with short hair increased one by

130

one. My aunt, when she saw me, had been as startled as if I had lost an arm. "In that shape, who would want you for a bride?" she had asked me. It seemed a long time ago that I, in high school, had hesitated even to wear my hair in actress hairdress. Now I was being reproved by a policeman for my appearance, and after he had gone, the children who lived in the small houses owned by the temple straggled after me. Occasionally they ran ahead of me, peering into my face with puzzled expressions, as if to say, "Is it a water-witch?" The water-witch in Japan is said to have short-cropped hair. When I looked at them, they ran away with choppy steps.

The following day was a clear May day. On the beach there was not even the shadow of man; blue sky and sea spread out to the very ends of the heavens. As I gazed at the sea my mind grew wings, and flew to an unknown land.

My friend lifted from my lap a volume of Taku-boku's poems and began to read in a low voice:

> On the white sand
> Of the shore
> On an island
> In the eastern sea
> Soaked in tears
> I played with a crab.

I cupped the fine white sand and let it fall through my fingers slowly. Unexpectedly, my friend told me that she was Korean.

I stared fixedly at her pale face. She used a Japanese name and spoke the language fluently, so that I had not had the slightest idea that she was Korean. Now that I had been told, I saw that her forehead was too high for a Japanese. Korea, which has a long history and an ancient culture, was annexed by Japan in 1910. From time to time Koreans, driven from their land and drifting like floating weeds, had come to the back entrance of our house with *furoshiki* packs on their shoulders. From the *furoshiki* they took out pencils, brushes and writing tablets and asked us in broken Japanese to buy them. Their frightened, tired eyes left a dark cloud in my mind, but always their departing figures had been those of strangers passing before my eyes.

My friend closed her eyes one moment. When she opened them they were wet with tears. I thought they would melt into my soul.

"Please don't tell this to anyone," she said. "The neighbors will complain to the temple if they find out we are Koreans."

She began to talk about the Mansai incident, which broke out the year after the ending of the World War, when the Koreans tried to regain their independence. Then she began to sing Korean songs in a calm voice. The tunes were sad and low, writhing inconsolably into the heart.

I slipped off my geta and stepped onto the wet sand. The tide was low, and the sea was lustrous like a mirror, stretching endlessly. Shells pale pink like women's fingernails and deep green pebbles washed by the waves, peeped from the sand. As I played with

132

the waves, chasing them, being chased by them, my friend's singing voice floated to my ears, drifting in the wind. And in my mind that voice resounds unceasingly. . . .

My Korean friend had graduated from a mission school in Korea, so she pronounced English correctly. But I, learning English from three Western ladies at Jiyu Gakuen, was bewildered because their pronunciations differed so much. One was an American lady about thirty years old, who wore long laced shoes, a white silk blouse, and a brown skirt. Another was a little old English lady, whose clothes were all different shades of purple. On her hat adorned with purple flowers she wore a thin veil like butterfly wings; and unlike the lively American lady, she was taciturn. The third Western lady taught dramatics. She did not understand Japanese at all, and she commuted to school in a jinrikisha. Under her thin black dress her white shoulders and arms rose softly, and her blue eyes looked especially blue in the white skin of her face. Under her direction we staged a Shakespeare play at Imperial Hotel. Many foreigners came to see it, but I don't know whether or not they understood our English.

The first year I spent in Jiyu Gakuen seemed both long and short. It seemed very long when I thought of all the things that had happened and all the incidents which had opened my mind. And yet the time seemed to flow away in an instant. Since Jiyu Gakuen was a new school, many well-known people as well as many unknown visitors came ceaselessly to observe

133

its methods. Students, guiding and informing them, began to know people, and learned to organize their own thoughts and feelings without being aware of it. When special lectures were given by well-known religious leaders, artists, or statesmen, we were called upon extempore to introduce the speaker or to make comments on the lecture before the audience. At first we could only blush; the words stuck in our throats.

My education until this time had trained me to accept whatever a teacher said—to swallow it whole like a cormorant, and repeat it like a parrot. At Jiyu Gakuen they laid emphasis on self-expression and the development of individuality. During my first year I stared wide-eyed, and breathed deeply of this new air.

But when the first year was over and I had been advanced to second year, doubt began to sprout in my mind. It became tiresome to go to the classroom and listen to lectures, and I sat alone under the wisteria arbor in the corner of the school yard. The wisteria was blooming in wild profusion as in the past year, and yellow butterflies were fluttering about; but from my mind the exhilarating feeling like fresh morning air had vanished.

I had come to Jiyu Gakuen yearning for freedom; but now it seemed to me that even here there was no true freedom. It was the purpose of Jiyu Gakuen to produce women rich in interests, intelligent and cultured. The observation of social work and the interviewing of notable people was not designed to train us for a profession, but merely to broaden our knowledge. Any serious consideration of what to do about

the social set-up was left to other people. To turn out
women who dressed with individual good taste, who
paid minute attention to the harmony of window
curtains and the placing of an ornament, who could
cook as well as talk about literature, music, painting
and general social questions—that was the ideal of
Jiyu Gakuen.

It seemed to me now that society was filled with
matters which needed to be deeply dug into, and I
suddenly came to a standstill before this "ideal."
What was the difference between this ideal woman
and the good wife and wise mother held up to us in
Girls' High School? I wondered if the old ideal had
not simply been dressed in new fragrance and modern color. If the finished product was to be a bright
social wife instead of a slave-wife, still the students
were being poured into a mold.

Thinking that this was a road that went far, I had
traveled along it briskly; but now a high wall obstructed my path. Vainly I stared at the corpse of
liberty that I held in my hands. I who had worshiped
Motoko Hani now felt like rising up against her
standards, good and bad. All those who sought small
ideals and small happiness looked insignificant to me.
And I, too, looked small and empty.

> *The smoke of Fuji*
> *Drifted by wind*
> *Vanishes in the sky.*
> *I know not my own*
> *Thought's destination. . . .*
> —Saigyo Hoshi

Earthquake

ON THE FIRST of September, 1923, I watched thick white clouds pile up in the shape of a dragon's head in the blue-cleared sky. Strong summer sunlight shining behind the clouds made folds of light and shadow. I knew that this was unusual for summer. The clouds which grew darker and darker and hurried with terrific speed across the sky entered into my spirit and stirred it to fear. The sunrays gleamed and then were extinguished, and rain pounded down, tearing the earth, cleansing every corner of the mind. Suddenly, from the very depths of the earth, terrible force rent the universe. The plaster fell from the walls and the house was filled with white smoke. I held my breath. My head, legs, hands, and soul were numbed. I sat dazed, fixed to the floor.

The gardener, his face twisted with worry, appeared and shouted, "Danger! Run to the garden!" I bounded like a ball from the veranda, and felt myself hurled into the center of the garden. I looked behind me. The house, always as firm as if it grew from the earth, was leaning to one side at a sharp angle. The servants and I stared at it, speechless. All at once it returned to its former position, like a man about to fall arching his back and regaining his balance. A cloud of dust rose near the fence as roof tiles from the neighbor's house fell into the garden. The waters of the little pool by which we were cowering came up in a wave like the surge of an angry ocean and spread over the lawn. Two goldfish, swept from the pool with the water, leaped in the green grass.

Father had left the evening before to go on a trip, and Younger Brother had left the house in the morning. Now Younger Brother returned home, panting. "Streetcars are stopped on the main street," he told us. "The street is filled with people who have fled from the side streets, and are sitting on mattresses and blankets they brought with them. I heard that three or four houses have fallen in Kanda and people are pinned under them."

The earthquake, which had subsided for a while, came back with earth-rending force, turning over our souls as we sat voiceless. Smaller quakes followed; then they too subsided. We shook off our numbness and began to move about. The watermains had burst, so we had to go to the well at the house next door and bring back water. The servants made a clay oven in the garden, for it was unsafe to go into a building.

They moved like shadows without spirit, and then, with Younger Brother and me, crouched forlornly among the bushes in the garden. Twilight stole uneasily over our lonely hearts. I wondered if Father and Elder Sister were safe.

Just as darkness fell, my aunt arrived with her household. Her garden was small, so she had brought her family to stay in our larger garden. The high voices of the children softened my heart which had been hardened to stone by fear. Aunt said, "On the way I saw crowds of people hurrying away with heavy burdens. They say that the fire is terrible downtown." As though suddenly unburdened, she dropped on the ground.

We dragged quilts out of the house into the garden, and made tents by stretching sheets from pine to pine. The white sheets gleamed through the darkness. I lay down on my back on my quilt and looked up at the sky. It was red, like spilled blood. A crescent moon, flat and unshining, hung between fingers of pine. My aunt's voice came through the darkness: "Fire. Flames reflected in the sky."

We slept fitfully. When I put my ear against the great earth I could hear, deep, deep, a growing-diminishing groan. The sky grew more and more red. By the time day whitely dawned, two-thirds of Tokyo had been devastated by the fire following the earthquake. A hundred and sixty thousand lives had been lost in the sea of flames.

The next day was long and fearful, with intermittent quakes. By nighttime a group of men had organized themselves into a voluntary corps of guards for the protection of property. Just at dusk we heard loud running footsteps, and Younger Brother appeared.

"Five hundred Koreans in Otsuka have set fire to a storehouse of explosives," he shouted excitedly.

The wavering flames of candles made small circles of dim light in the garden. Aunt's face, only partly visible in the candle light, grew pale. For a while no one spoke. The leaves of trees rustled into stillness. Then the maid said, "When I went to get water from the well, they were saying Koreans are putting poison in wells and we must be careful. Isn't it terrible?"

I could not see the maid. I could only hear her voice in the darkness. Just then I heard men among the trees between the neighbor's house and ours. All of us looked in that direction, our eyes straining into the darkness as though following the footsteps. Aunt's trembling, cold hand reached over and grasped mine. The faint glow of lantern light filtered from the deep dark of a cluster of trees. Younger Brother called, "*Oye!*"

The sound seemed wrung from his throat, pushed out by his consciousness of being the only man in a group of women. "*Oye!*"

"It's I." The familiar voice of our gardener came from the thicket, joined by other, strange voices. They told us that they had come to investigate a report that there were some Koreans in the neighborhood. "But it's all right. Please be at ease," they yelled. The faint light of their lantern wavered in the darkness and disappeared.

139

"Koreans, they say, take explosives and set fires from roof to roof," Younger Brother said in fear-choked voice, peering up at our roof as though he saw there black, invisible figures.

Aunt looked at my face. I felt sure that Koreans would not do such a thing. I said, in as calm a voice as I could muster, "Such things are rumors spread by someone. Koreans are just like us, suffering from calamity like us. They too are in great trouble. I don't believe these stories can be so."

A strong gust of wind blew out our candles. In the pitch-blackness we heard someone running, and Aunt's manservant called out breathlessly, "I just saw a police notice. It said that wicked Koreans with dangerous weapons are all about, pillaging, setting fires, putting poison in wells. Take care, it said. On the way home I saw a crowd gathered. A suspicious-looking Korean was being thrashed. I heard his shrieking, 'Ki! Ki!' His shirt was tattered."

I was troubled, not knowing how to explain to the others that this must be a falsehood. Aunt's manservant shuddered, and went on: "By mistake, some Japanese were also thrashed. There are vigilantes at the corners of the streets. When they ask, 'Who goes there?' and you can't remember right off your name and address, and you stutter, they beat you up, thinking you're a Korean."

Aunt's baby, frightened by a dream, cried out in his sleep. Aunt, perturbed, hurried into the tent. Everyone was silent, speech forgotten. Only the baby's wailing sounded sorrowfully in the bushes.

140

Even that ended, and uneasiness and dead silence filled the depths of our souls. My mind, sad at being unable to free the Koreans of guilt, wandered in darkness.

During the shortage of food that followed the earthquake, Seiken Yamaguchi of the Constitutional Labor Party took the responsibility of opening Government storehouses in Yokohama and distributing foodstuffs to the victims of earthquake and fire. It was reported by the police of Yokohama that Koreans had set fire to the storehouses. On the strength of this report, four thousand Koreans were killed in Tokyo.

We spent three days and three nights in our garden as the earthquake continued. We were fortunate in having a sufficient store of food; most families were not so fortunate. We learned that Elder Sister and all of our relatives were safe. Our only concern then was for Father, who was on a tour of inspection in the western part of Japan. We felt certain that he was safe in that region; but we knew how worried he must be about us, for the first news sent over the world was that Tokyo had been completely demolished and that not one life had been saved. We sent daily telegrams to Father, but lines of communication were cut off, and it was not until the sixth night that we had a reply from him. I held his telegram against the faint candle light and read and re-read his message: "News Tokyo demolished. Spent day after day worrying. Just now learned of your safety. This peace of mind inestimable."

After a while our candles were used up, and there

141

were no more to be had. We put rapeweed oil in a small saucer around a thick cord of dried rush. This we used for several days. One evening, as I was watching this sputtering light, I heard Younger Brother come into the house, stumbling over the geta in the *genkan*. Sixteen-year-old Brother, proud of being in the Voluntary Corps, brought us news of the happenings in town.

Now, with round eyes, he said, "I heard just now that Socialists have rioted and rushed on the Imperial palace. They say that it was Socialists who incited the Koreans. They say that thousands of Socialists have been arrested and some of them killed." He drank a cup of water and rushed away again.

That evening as I stood at the gate, gazing toward town, I saw a company of soldiers march up, as if to battle, their bayonets gleaming over their shoulders. I shivered. That cold gleam of bayonets still lives in my memory. My mind was troubled and my heart torn by the many rumors passing from lip to lip.

It was learned much later that the rumor about the Socialists attacking the palace had sprung from the fact that the crowd, driven out of their homes by flames, had sought shelter in the dark-forested palace grounds, and had been driven away by the Imperial guard. But immediately after the incident, before the truth was known, thirteen hundred people thought to be harboring dangerous thoughts were arrested. Nine labor leaders who were being held in the detention prison of Kameido were taken out behind the building and stabbed one by one with bayonets. I heard

142

the rumor that Sakai Osugi, a Socialist leader, had also been killed, but I could not believe it. He was held in great estimation, not only because of his generous aid to people in need, but also because of his contribution to letters. I had heard him lecture only a month before, and his large, dewy-black eyes were still vivid in my memory. I tried to erase the report of his death from my mind, but I could not forget it. From the depths of my soul I prayed for his safety.

My school, taking part in earthquake relief work, sent us one morning to the hospitals to comfort the friendless victims there. On the way I opened a newspaper and saw a notice that Osugi, his wife, and his nephew, had indeed been killed by police when they were returning from the home of Osugi's brother. The news was like a blow in the center of my brain. The three bodies had been hidden in an abandoned well and piled over with rocks. There was a picture showing the well and the details of the murder. The victims had been strangled. Looking at that blurred picture, I felt beyond the newspaper and beyond the picture something I could not fathom. I could see the thick arms of the police and feel their fingers tighten around my throat. Darkness descended before my eyes, as though suddenly I had walked from sunlight into a shadowed room. I could not brush it away. In this fumbling-in-dark-forest mood, I reached the hospital.

On the bare wooden floors were rows and rows of thin cotton pads. Patients, so swathed in bandages that only their faces were visible, lay on the pads

143

spiritlessly and stared up blankly at the ceiling. I was filled with cold horror. I stood at the door, unable to move; my legs felt as though they would draw up. Groans and sniffling cries came from various parts of the room. A thin plaint, "*Kangofu-san*—Miss Nurse!" rose and threaded through the bare hall. Then again, gathering strength, "*Kangofu-san!*" But there was no white-uniformed nurse in sight. A woman lying at my feet looked up at me casually and said, "That poor man! He's the only one alive of his family of nine. All alone, without anyone—like me."

These were the only survivors of three hundred and fifty thousand people of the poorer section who had escaped from their hovels to take refuge in an open lot. The buildings around the lot and the possessions they had brought with them had caught fire, and the place had turned into a furnace. Only about a hundred of the people had been saved, and they had been crowded together in this hospital. Seeing them after their frightful experiences, I felt that I, who had known such secluded safety, could not understand their suffering. I had no words to say to them. Anything I could say would seem thin-sheer.

Leaving the hospital, I descended the hill. From its slope I could see the devastated waste of the city, with nothing to obstruct my vision to the far horizon. Ashes and burnt refuse rose up in smoke-whirls. I felt a gritty taste in my mouth. On the side of the hill a woman with a printed towel wrapped around her head poked among cinders with a stick. Her turbaned head stood out sharply from the uniform gray

144

of burned waste. What was she seeking? Perhaps she had come to revisit her old home, feeling that the soul of her lost child might be wandering among the ruins. Here and there along the street concrete structures protruded like battlements, their windows black.

In Hirokōji Square, at the bottom of the hill, several women sitting near a desk were distributing circulars. On the desk was a book in which people were writing. I wondered what this was about. As I approached, one of the ladies handed me a circular, and I discovered that they were representatives of a federation of women's organizations which were petitioning against the rebuilding of Yoshiwara, the red-light district, and for the complete abolition of licensed prostitution. I bowed to the gray-haired lady at the desk and entered my name on the register.

As I left the Square, I remembered that not one prostitute had escaped from Yoshiwara. Locked in their cells, like the birds in a cage to which they are compared, they had every one been burned alive.

I turned left toward Uyeno Park, which was like an oasis in the gray desert. It seemed to me as I walked that a catastrophe like an earthquake was a natural, inevitable one which could not be avoided. But I wondered if something could not be done about the tragedy left in its wake. Newspaper articles told of progressive foreign cities with as much as 10 per cent park space, 30 per cent street pace. In Tokyo there was only 2½ per cent park space and 10 per cent street space. If Tokyo had been built differently, would not the damage have been considerably less?

145

Ascending the stone steps of Uyeno Hill, I looked beyond far Sumida River, shining like a silver ribbon. Before the earthquake, factory chimneys had lined its banks like a forest. Now there was not even a wisp of smoke on the gray flat land. In that section, as in Yoshiwara, many girls and women had been burned alive. When they rushed out of the walls surrounding the burning factories, they had been thrust back by guards who told them that they had been bought and that their lives were not their own. I had heard that most of the emergency exits had been locked, so that the women were unable to escape.

Looking over the vast desolate waste, and thinking of these unfortunate and ill-fated people, I felt a withering, wintry storm raging within my heart.

The sun, larger and redder than I had ever seen it, was setting on the western horizon. My native city bowed low before it, as if lamenting; as if it bowed in long and thoughtful prayer to its loved, lost souls.

Visiting Kobe-Shinkawa Slums

DELIBERATELY wearing dark simple kimono of coarse silk and carrying a wicker basket and one book, I boarded an electric train going to Kobe. The book was Kagawa's *Shisen wo Koete* (*Beyond Death*), filled with his love for the unfortunate people. To me whose mind was wandering in darkness, it was like a gleam of light. I placed the book on my knees, and my hands upon it, resting gently. I would have drawn its thought into my soul, to enfold and impress it there.

The rain had been falling heavily when I left my grandmother's house in Osaka where I had been visiting for several days. Now the sky had cleared. Outside the train window, light rays burst suddenly over peach orchards and pierced through clouds of pink peach blossoms. The flat white adobe houses lay like scattered petals across the countryside. Far away a range of hills, gently sloping like a woman's breast, rose up in purplish haze.

Grandmother's supplicating voice still rang in my ears: "When it is raining so hard, why are you leaving the house? It would be better to postpone it, *ne?*"

With all her will and overflowing love she had tried to keep me with her. And in my love for her was heartfelt anguish that though my body was near her, my mind was far away. The I reflected in my grandmother's eye-pupil was an innocent, grandmother's-word-obediently-receiving, dreaming-to-be-flower-bride I. But I had pushed her supplication out of my mind and left her house in the rain.

Sitting in the oily-smelling kuruma, completely enclosed by oilcloth, I had listened lonesomely to the raindrops on the hood and felt my heart throbbing with pain at having cut off Grandmother's affection. But now, as the soothing breeze blew over me from the window, I knew that Grandmother's love like arms outstretched could no longer embrace my wandering, troubled heart. I thought it well that I had left her house to visit Kagawa in his Kobe-Shinkawa slums.

Quietly I took up the book from my knees and began turning the pages. The great, comprehending love of the man who had crawled into the dark dampness of poverty spoke to me in my heart. I thought of the slums to which we had been taken by the Higher Girls' School: eyes glittering and glaring out of the deeps of darkness; cries of infants, beginning

148

and rebeginning; ash-colored tatters of the shoji fluttering with a sobbing sound. . . . It seemed to me
that strangers—everyone, even these people in the
slums—had some object in life, some reason for living, some direction. I alone lived without significance,
without meaning, like a *mushi* parasite.

When I alighted from the train into the dusty
streets of Kobe, the high summer sun was beating
down. The houses in the town, the train, the rails,
looked as if they would melt in its shining. I took
out Kagawa's letter once more, and re-read the difficult directions to his house. Following them, I turned
a corner, twice crossed the hot-burning railroad,
rounded the corner with the tobacconist's red sign-
board, and at last looked for Kagawa's home in the
narrow alley.

Going upstairs, away from the hot streets, I felt
the inside coolness wind-smooth in the center of my
brain.

In the middle of Kagawa's room was a desk, on
top of which lay scattered books and papers. Although
it was a matted Japanese room, it was partly Occidental, with a few cheap wooden chairs. I sat in a
chair in the corner and looked quietly about, trying
to form an image of the person from his room. There
were no ornaments; only an electric light with a flat
conical shade hung from the center of the ceiling.
The doors of the closet in the hall had been removed
and the shelves were completely filled with books.

As I picked up from the desk the magazine *Pillar
of Cloud,* and started opening its pages, I heard a

149

creak-creak on the stairs, and Toyohiko Kagawa entered the room. He wore gray uncreased trousers and a cotton-mixed jacket that looked as though it had been starched. The roundness of his face was emphasized by the black bandage on one eye. His good eye was rimmed with red, as though the entering light hurt it. Living and working in the slums, he had contracted trachoma; once there had been danger that the other eye would also go. In the presence of such an esteemed person, the things I was going to say, the questions I was going to ask, were tangled in my throat, and I was speechless. At his suggestion, I followed him into the slum alley.

In the slums were nests of paupers, former criminals, beggars, prostitutes, drug and alcohol addicts—the wrecks and dregs of society. The sorrows and sighs of the defeated, forgotten by the world, lay stagnant in this heavy air. On both sides of the alley, hovels, half-buried, slanted into the ground. Families of from five to ten persons lived huddled in houses six feet square. For about every thirty houses there was a community kitchen and a community toilet. The ground under foot was sodden with water thrown from the houses, and as we walked along the alley the water oozed under our feet.

Two or three children jumped out from a corner.

"*Sensei*, teacher," they cried. Their faces and hands were covered with grime.

"What is this? Such dirty faces!" Kagawa laughed.

A girl child, looking at me, seemed to think sud-
150

denly of her dirty face, and wiped it with the right sleeve of her dress.

Gradually more children appeared, shuffling along beside us, peering and staring into my face. We went through twisted alleys and came to a small vacant lot. Facing this lot was a slightly larger building, with a frosted glass sliding shutter gleaming white among the sooty surroundings. The late afternoon sun struck it slantingly, making it seem transparent and tinged with blue.

"This is the dispensary," Kagawa said. "Let us enter and see."

The glass shutter clattered loudly as we went in, and the strong odor of medicine pushed into our noses. After the bad odor of the slums, this smell was like a restorative.

There were rows of benches in the waiting room, and people sitting there: a mother, exposing her large breasts, suckling her baby; like a green gourd, the face of a small boy; a young woman with dry, wrinkled skin; an old man with protruding cheek bones. When Kagawa appeared, their voices rose spontaneously: "*Ara ma! Sensei!*" The old man, seized with a fit of coughing, bowed his head and mumbled in his throat.

Soon we left the dispensary and went on to the section where about twenty thousand Eta were living. In Japan there are about three million of this outcast class, rejected by society and forced to live in their own sections in extreme poverty. There are various conjectures as to their origin. One is that they

151

were fugitives from Korea around the seventh century. Long ago the slaughter of animals and the curing of hides, the most menial tasks according to Buddhist teachings, were relegated to them. During the Meiji Restoration (1868) the class of outcasts was officially abolished and re-named "newcommoner." But socially the discrimination remained, and there was no intermarriage or even ordinary social intercourse with other groups. The literal meaning of the word *eta* is "dirt, filth." They are also called "four-legged."

Kagawa told me: "Even now people feel the Eta are filthy. When an Eta comes to an ordinary shop, they sprinkle salt after him to purify the place. Once when I was in this section I stopped about mealtime in the home of an Eta and shared his meal of rice with tea and pickles. The Eta sitting around exclaimed joyfully, 'Ah, *Sensei* has eaten the rice of our household!' Usually no one will cross the threshold of an Eta house. So that my eating the food of their house greatly rejoiced them."

One by one the houses withdrew in the twilight, as though sinking in gray lumps into the damp earth. As I silently followed Kagawa along the alleys, I thought of his poem about Shinkawa: *

One month in the slums,
　　And I am sad,
　　　So sad

* From *Songs from the Slums,* interpretation by Lois J. Erickson.

I seem devil-possessed,
Or mad.
Sweet heaven sends
No miracle
To ease
This hell;
The careless earth
Rings no
Alarum bell.
But here there are slippery streets which never are
dry;
They are lined with open sewers, where rats come out
to die;
Tattered paper doors stand wide to winds that beat;
The houses are all of a reddish black, like the hue of
stale whale meat;
Filth on the flimsy ceilings, dirt in the musty air;
Elbowed out of their crowded rooms, people are every-
where—
All night long they crouch in the cold, huddled on
broken benches,
Where there's never a moment's lifting of the heavy
offal stenches.

Although I had spent only a few hours in the slums, already I felt that poverty's dark heaviness, issuing from the earth unendingly, was shriveling my heart.

At supper time Kagawa said, "If you really want to test yourself, you might go tonight to the slum bathhouse. Do you have the mind to go?"

A cold shiver ran down my spine at the idea of

going to a public bathhouse of the diseased. But, I
thought, if I am frightened at such things, what can
I hope to accomplish here? If I am human, so are
these slum-dwellers. The bath they enter, I can enter.
So I reprimanded my fearing heart.

When supper was finished, I was taken by Madame
Kagawa to the public bath. In a public bathhouse
there is one large sunken wooden tub filling a large
part of the room. In this everyone bathes at the same
time, after being splashed with water from a basin.
By nine o'clock, even in an ordinary public bathhouse, the oily dirt from bodies floats on the surface
of the water like scum. Here, I could not help feeling, it would be even dirtier than waste water.

Standing in the bathroom foggy with steam, I
closed my eyes and resolutely put one leg into the
tub. As my foot touched the bottom of the wooden
tub, I felt the smeary slime. The warm water came
only to my chest. In the tub were many blurred, squat-
ting forms, with only the blackness of hair floating
clear over the surface of the water.

Gradually faces emerged. Madame Kagawa, as
though swimming, went around the tub greeting
people. In the *nagashiba*, the sponging-off place, the
naked red bodies of women moved mistily in the
white steam. The splashing of bodies went on with
an endless water sound. Mingled with it were the
high-pitched laughing voices of the women, as they
washed each other's backs in friendly fashion. In the
next room was the men's bath. The singing and recita-
tive of the *naniwabushi* and *gidayu*, narrative songs,

154

came floating over the partition. The women on their side tittered at the sound. For these people the public bathhouse was a pleasant meeting place, a community center for the slums.

When we left the bathhouse, the summer night breeze blew softly over the bathed, relaxed forms on the road returning. Along the alleys the women squatted in white undershirts with only one hip wrapper, cooling off, keeping away mosquitoes with slap of fans in the darkness.

"*Konban wa,* good evening!" Madame Kagawa greeted them, bending her knees as she passed along.

I, carrying my soap in wet towel, bowed too, as though stumbling over stone, following the bowing form of Madame Kagawa.

That night I slept in a small two-mat room, which was almost completely filled by the quilt. My body resting on the thin quilt hurt suddenly, as if all the bones protruded. Madame Kagawa's half-laughing words as she left me came back into my mind: "*Nankin* insects, bedbugs, might come out." I could feel my legs and shoulders crawl.

Could I endure this slum living, I wondered, like Madame Kagawa who was so completely absorbed in it? I tossed on the thin quilt, my thought continuing. I had come to the slums with heroic feeling, determined to be selfless. Seeking direction in living, I had come here to work. But the reality had shattered by romantic feeling. In thinking to make myself selfless for the slums, I had considered the slums, not on a level with me, but below me. Could I fuse my

155

mind and body into this existence? For Madame Kagawa, slum life had seeped into every corner of her being, until no part of her was alien to it. Could I be like that?

The deep night, everyone sleep-calmed, was still as a forest. Only my tossing shattered the silence. Over and over I asked myself the same question, like one who is lost in a forest and traveling the same circular path.

Hunting for a Job

ONE NIGHT after supper, Father, pulling the smoking tray toward him, took up a pipe and began serenely to blow out purplish smoke. After two or three puffs he emptied the pipe, with a hollow knocking sound, into the bamboo ash container, and refilled the bowl with fresh tobacco. I, reading the evening newspaper, heard the tap-tap of the pipe as if from far away.

The newspaper was filled with news of general manhood suffrage, which had been pending for several years, and which had just been passed by both Houses. This was the spring of 1925, and until this time only those who paid an income tax of ten yen had been permitted to vote. By the new law the electorate was increased four and a half times; therefore it was predicted that the Non-Propertied Party would

157

gain tremendous strength. The previous night I had attended the organizational meeting of the Non-Propertied Party. As I read and recollected that meeting, Father spoke to me, in ceremonious voice, "Haru!"

Quickly I took my eyes from the newspaper.

"If you are not busy, please come upstairs to my study for a moment." With these words he left me and ascended the stairs, his footsteps making a *tonton* sound. The sound seeped into my soul; it was as if the steps were walking up the many, many stairs of my mind. Then, as the sound faded overhead, I collected my thoughts.

Probably Father was going to say something about my having returned home late last night. I had gone to the meeting without his permission, and had returned home around twelve o'clock. From the gate, over the graveled path, I had walked softly, setting one foot cautiously before the other. The outer shutter of the *genkan* had been slightly open, and lifting it with both hands I had slipped inside. No ray of light leaked out of Father's study into the spreading darkness. The house was settled in sleep; there was not even a sound of anyone turning in sleep. Sighing with relief, I had gone into my bedroom.

Now, mounting the stairs one by one, leisurely, deliberately, I thought of Father's formal tone of voice. That tone was like a weight on my head. Had I wronged Father in any way? Although I had gone out without his permission and had returned late, searching my heart I could find no disgrace in this. Father might try to hold me in his own world, but

158

my heart, like a small bird which had spread its wings, was flying about in the great wide sky. Even though he was my father, he could not put the bird back again in a narrow cage. Even if in my soaring my wings should be crushed and broken and my head bruised against jagged mountain crags, I was determined to endure the suffering, alone and in silence. Saying in my heart, "Father, please let me fly free," I crossed the threshold of his study.

At the entrance of the room was the huge table which had been placed in the dining room when we were children, and which later had become an encumbrance. It almost filled up Father's study, as it had filled up the dining room. I sat down at the side of the table, my hands folded on my knees.

Sitting with head bowed, Father said gently, "Since I am away from home a great deal and you do not have a mother, I always feel sorry for you, Haru. A family without a mother has no leaning place; it is a lonely one. Elder Sister who has gone as bride and Oba-san have always blamed me for allowing you too much freedom. They say you act wilfully. But because I thought you gadded about because you had no mother and were lonely, I could not say anything to you. I could not blame you."

Preparing for the scolding which I thought Father would give me, I had built up a wall in my mind; but now, at the mention of Mother, the wall crumbled inside me. I felt as though my heart tightened, and then filled to overflowing. I clenched my hands folded on my knees and closed my eyes. Outside the rain

159

was falling gently on the leaves. Its steady patter stole into my mind, awakening the dews of tears.

Father went on, "Haru, if your mother had lived, perhaps you would have grown up home-like, like other girls. Second Mother too is gone. Many unfortunate things have happened, *ne?* In order to fill this empty loneliness you have gone outside the home, pulled by other interests. From time to time I think, if only you were a boy! In that case I could let you do a little more as you desire, according to your will. But, Haru, please consider carefully what you are doing. . . ."

I sat silently, without voice.

That night as I lay in bed staring into the darkness, Father's words floated back to me again and again: "Haru, please consider carefully. . . ." Night deepened and the footsteps of rain grew stronger. The wind rose and blew, sometimes with a groaning, sometimes with an angry scolding sound. Rain beating against the shutter seemed to beat and dash against my head, resounding loudly. Should I heed my father's words? Should I cast away my own will so as not to worry him? Was it a daughter's duty to fold the outspread wings and return to the cage in order to ease a father's anxiety? Into my mind came peacefully the image of Elder Sister gone as fortunate bride. Elder Sister's life was like a lake among mountains, eternal, unflowing, without one wave; it had no connection with the world's torrent. But in my mind mighty waves were dashing. Even though I tried to shut out the whirling current of the world,

160

it rushed in, shaking and moving me. Was Father saying to me, "Do not listen to this flow"? In the darkness his face appeared before me. It seemed to say, "I understand your feeling; but consider Father's mind which cannot allow it."

One day about a month later I went resolutely to the office of a lady's magazine in answer to a newspaper advertisement for a writer. I had decided that if I could earn my own living I would be relieved of the mental burden of being unable to obey my father's wishes. Then too, if I could do this I might more easily escape relatives' criticism. After I arrived at this conclusion, I looked over the employment columns, which I had never done before, and found this advertisement for a magazine writer.

Outside the office door on the third floor of the Kanda Building, I hesitated. Should I withdraw, or should I determinedly enter? My two minds argued the question. Footsteps approached in the corridor, and hurriedly I knocked on the door.

The room I entered had the empty look of a vacant room. Two middle-aged men, who did not seem to know much courtesy, sat facing each other across two desks. The desks were full of ink stains, and the paint had worn off the corners. Old newspapers and scrap papers were piled on top of them in great confusion. The chairs on which the men sat were a soiled white; there were only two chairs in the room. Waste papers and butt ends of cigarettes were strewn over the floor. I stood rooted in the middle of the room. Could this be the office of a magazine publisher? Looking at the crude scene, I wondered if I had come to the wrong place.

The man with gold-rimmed glasses took my references, glanced over them, handed them to the other man, then turned toward me. His eyes gleamed in the depths of glasses as he stared at me from head to foot. Cold and insolent, they seemed to freeze my mind. Was the independent life I was seeking to be found icily sprawling in such a place as this? I felt a dizziness; darkness swallowed me up.

Through the dizziness, my inattentive ear heard these words: "Since we are just starting the magazine, we cannot pay more than twenty yen a month salary. But if you will be patient for two or three months, we will increase it."

Twenty yen a month salary. I left in a half-daze, and reached the main street in Kanda district. There as usual everything was confusion—streetcars squealing, traffic whistles blowing. Today the jarring of the cars, the sound of geta, seemed to scoff at me. I felt a sudden self-pity, as though I, thrown into an unfriendly universe, walked my lonely way forlornly. Where was the determination to show them I could live an independent life? The sky was threateningly clouded. It looked like rain. The cold, ashen heavens closed around my mind.

I had brought two newspaper clippings with me when I left the house: one about the fake magazine, the other about a position as secretary to a gentleman returned from America and residing at Imperial Hotel. Unexpected good fortune might await me if

162

I answered the second advertisement. I stood before Imperial Hotel, bolstering up my crushed spirit. Once on the stage in this hotel I had had a role in Shakespeare's play, *Midsummer Night's Dream*. We had produced the play in order to raise funds for the school, Jiyu Gakuen, and at that time I had come to the hotel every day. These memories thawed out my frozen heart.

The gentleman from America, unlike the magazine editors, was extremely courteous and gentle in words and bearing. He said, "As to the salary . . ."

I had been feeling that I would not mind working in a place like this, and so I leaned forward, waiting for his next word.

"That," he said, "I cannot pay for a little while. But it will be only for about a month. If business begins to take shape, I will pay you an appropriate amount. You are a cultured young lady from a fine family, and I am fortunate indeed to procure the services of such a person."

At first I doubted my own ears. Surely it was impossible that he would ask me to work for him without pay. My face must have clouded, for the gentleman said, "Don't worry; it will be only in the beginning." As if to gloss the matter over, he gave an artificial laugh. "You will be the ideal person, you know. Even in the advertisement I specified that a person without family ties need not apply." He puffed leisurely on his cigar.

Feeling weak and confused, as if I had been dropped from a high wall, I left the hotel. Outside

163

a light rain fell soundlessly. The silent dampness was like a heavy hand upon my shoulders. The thicket of trees in Hibiya Park misted in the rain and floated like a Sumiye water color. The willows, heavy with rain, drooped their thin silver stems. My heart, heavy with rain, felt as though it were sinking into the depths of the earth. The pale street lights cast glimmering shadows on the wet walk. People were returning from work, bustling through the twilight streets, making a living, criss-cross brocade. A woman followed me, passed me. I saw the worn geta on her hurrying feet, and, raising my eyes, I saw the seam of her obi frayed to tatters. All around me the shabby forms of working women moved in an endless, running, flowing-withdrawing stream. They who were living by work, buffeted by the world's rough waves— were they not more worthy than I? I looked deeply into myself. I did not even know how to earn my own livelihood. Already, before the rough winds of the world had touched me, I was so tired. I felt as though my body were shrinking with sorrow, as though it wanted to cry. . . .

Several months later, through an introduction from an acquaintance, I found work in a small private office which published an educational journal for elementary school teachers. I had found, during these months, that it was almost impossible to depend on newspaper advertisements in looking for work.

This magazine office was really a part of the owner's residence. In the mornings, as I opened the outer shutter and entered the *genkan,* his smallest boy,

164

aged four, would run out and greet me. I took off my geta and put them away on the geta shelf. If I neglected to do this, the child and the dog would take them to the corners of the garden, and when it was time for me to go home the geta could not be found and there was great confusion. The room in which I worked faced north and was somewhat damp, but it looked out on a small garden when the shoji was opened, and it was quiet.

Mr. Kinoshita, the owner of the journal, was a devout protagonist of suffrage for women. He was also very idealistic. Perhaps his idealism made it possible for me to work without too much blundering even though I was inexperienced. At noon I was invited to his living quarters for lunch. His shriveled, skin-and-bone wife served her husband and me silently, sitting near our table.

"This afternoon," Mr. Kinoshita said, "Miss Kawada, the feminist, is arriving. Now that universal manhood suffrage is the law, she will agitate to get woman suffrage passed by the next Diet. She wants our magazine to appeal to the women teachers."

"Shall I take care of that article?" I asked.

"Yes, I'll ask you to do that, since you have an interest along that line. When you meet Miss Kawada, you will find that you have things in common, I am sure."

Miss Kawada was one of the "new women" we had so fearfully heard about in our childhood. I was thinking about those childhood impressions when Mr. Kinoshita called to his wife in a loud, scolding

165

voice: "Oi, hey! Tea! Tea! What makes you so slow?"

His wife, who had been standing in the kitchen, excitedly picked up the teapot and brought it in.

Sipping that tea, I thought about the wife standing and working all day, with no voice, not even the sound of footsteps, to indicate her presence. And I observed with wonderment the tyrannical attitude of Mr. Kinoshita. Is this the way a man advocating freedom and rights of women should treat his wife? I wondered if the ancient attitude toward women had seeped so thoroughly into the male mind that even in a man with understanding of women's problems it could not be wiped away.

After lunch that day I read the newspaper at my desk. The question of women's rights was being discussed so loudly in the world that this newspaper had collected opinions from women readers. I read some of the opinions in the woman's column: "It is necessary to eradicate from the male mind the idea that man is master and woman is slave." "Woman seeks freedom." "Same education for women as for men, same civil rights, same pay for same kind of work." "Although the Japanese kimono is beautiful to look at, it is a great hindrance to our activities."

I thought of my salary, which was only thirty-five yen a month. The work I had finally succeeded in getting in order not to worry my father was not even enough to sustain me alone.

That evening in the crowded streetcar, I gazed at the form of the woman sitting next to me, shaken by the car, her legs and arms stretched out as if they were too heavy for her; and the woman standing in front of me, hanging on the strap. Looking at the torn and tattered edge of her sleeve, I felt that for the first time I was learning about the world. The pupils of my mind were opened, and suffering and sorrow and struggle vibrated into my heart.

The Intelligence Officer

EVEN AFTER I went to bed the incidents of the day whirled through my mind, and I could not fall asleep. The feeling that a heavy burden had been lifted and the feeling that I had done a terribly stupid thing chased each other round and round in my brain. When I thought of myself standing and speaking in that lecture hall crowded to overflowing, I felt my cheeks burn. Try as I would, I could not remember how I had looked or what I had said on the platform. Only the applause as I descended from it in a daze remained faintly in my ears. I changed my position in bed, hoping to sleep; under my breath I repeated, "It's finished." I could hear from outside the *kachi-kachi* sound made by the night-watchman as he walked by tapping his wooden clappers. But when I closed my eyes, the scene in the

168

lecture hall came back as though spotlighted. Then other scenes appeared, flickeringly, as if from a magic lantern.

The meeting had been sponsored by *Woman and Labor,* a magazine published by a feminist agitator. This was 1927, and I was now an unpaid worker for the magazine. For this meeting I had prepared and memorized and practiced a five-minute talk explaining the purposes of the magazine. Lying in bed I remembered how, after time for the opening of the meeting, the speakers had not all assembled, and I had been at my wit's end; I had worked hard to find a substitute for the notable man from the Fabian Society who, at the last minute, had been unable to come; the heckling voices of the audience and the clapping hands urging the opening of the meeting had wrung my body with agony. All these things came back endlessly to my sleepless mind. I relived the hour before the meeting when the rain had begun to fall from the clouded sky, and we had gazed bitterly at the heavens. But in spite of the rain, perhaps because it was unusual to have a meeting sponsored by women, the audience had come in great numbers. There had been a scarcity of chairs. One by one the recollections unwound like a thread in my mind. . . .

For a long time I had been living as though enclosed in mist, turning first this way then that way, finding no road to follow. The thought that in order to live I must do something useful, rested heavily on my head; but I had no idea of what I should do. I asked myself why I was living. Seeking some light to show me my way, I wandered in starless and moonless dark. Then I began doing a little work for *Woman and Labor,* and it seemed to me that a faint light was cast upon my path. Just as a coal miner feels the answer to his hand when his pick strikes a vein of coal, so I finally had found some answer to my search for a meaning in existence.

Far away the temple bell rang twice, *gon-gon.* I got out of bed and slid back the casement shoji. The rain had stopped. A pale moon behind a light gray cloud went glidingly across the sky. The early spring night wind laden with dew was cool to my burning cheeks. The young spring leaves exuded a smothering fragrance. I breathed deeply, and that fragrance seeped into the core of my brain, smoothing out the tired wrinkles there. Then I thought of the discussion meeting to be held tomorrow and of the criticisms that would be made of tonight's meeting, and my cheeks burned again. Since the earthquake, about twenty young women had begun to assemble each Sunday to discuss social problems. When Father was away they met at my house.

The cloud across the moon thinned gradually, and the spring moonlight shone clear. It flowed into my room, over the Sumiye hanging which Mother had painted before she became a bride, and which I had begged of my grandmother for a keepsake. This hanging brought my mother's fragrance close to me. Pallidly disclosed by the moon, it was like her dead face, pale and clear. It gave me a pure and noble feeling.

Next morning the air was crystal-clear. Over the
170

dining room eaves plum blossoms bloomed along the branch; their perfume filled the room. Now the memory of last night was only the memory of a duty done, and my mind and body melted into the fragrance of the plum blossoms. For the first time in a long while I had a feeling of leisure; I thought I would like to arrange flowers, and I stepped onto the veranda with garden shears. A *uguisu* bird began singing "*ho hokekyo*" from the plum branch. I sat down on the veranda so as not to disturb him. The singing voice seemed to issue from a gentle, new-born throat: "*kekyo kekyo*" it sang excitedly, like an infant with faltering tongue. Just then the bell at the side *genkan* rang resoundingly, breaking the peaceful scene. The *uguisu,* frightened by the sound, suddenly stopped his song.

It was very rare to have visitors on Sunday, even when Father was at home. I was thinking that it was either a peddler or a priest of Hachiman Shrine bringing his book for collections or his bag for rice, when the maid who had answered the bell said that it was a guest for me. Lightly straightening my obi, I went to the *genkan*. The man standing there was someone I had never seen before. He wore a well-pressed Western suit, and over it a silver-gray spring topcoat; in his right hand he carried a soft felt hat of the same color. As I sat on the matted floor of the *genkan,* he placed his hat on the wide wooden step and took a visiting card out of his pocket. Without any premonition of danger I dropped my eyes to the card; I saw

171

the words "Intelligence Officer" written in bigger type than the name.

"Eh, it is nothing important. I came merely to call your attention to certain things." The officer smirked, revealing his front gold teeth. Without invitation he seated himself on the step and obliquely faced me. The positions of host and guest seemed to be completely reversed. His attitude was calm; I sat, with tense body, like a mouse being watched by a cat.

"Last night's meeting was a big success, wasn't it?" He puffed at his cigarette, the pupils of his eyes glittering.

The speakers at the meeting last night, he went on to say, and all of the notables of the Fabian Society were possessors of dangerous thought. It would be harmful for me to associate with such people. "Don't you think it will be to your advantage not to mingle with them?" he said. "You are the daughter of an educator. Isn't there a saying that a wise person never approaches danger?" He used extremely courteous words, and treated me like an innocent and ignorant girl. I wanted to reply to his words, which seemed to be dropping from above and wrapping me up, but I checked my impulse and sat silently, watching my opponent's face.

"Ha-ha-ha-ha!" The officer's empty laugh sounded as though he were mocking himself. He leaned toward me with the manner of one conferring a favor, and said that this time he would consider my welfare and keep my activities a secret. "You are of the age to be married, *ne?* It would be a calamity if you be-

172

came 'damaged goods.' If you frequent such meetings, no one will want you for a bride. Wouldn't it be terrible if you couldn't become a bride? You will be careful from now on, *ne?*"

"That's true," I said, purposely appearing stupid. The restless waves in my mind felt as though they would dash into my face.

"As the adage goes, 'If you mix with scarlet, you will become red.' It's important to choose your acquaintances."

Then he asked about the discussion group that met at my house on Sundays. He said, "If these people come and go from your house in great numbers, your reputation in the neighborhood will become unsavory." He repeated two or three such admonitions as he leisurely finished his cigarette. Then he got up. "So then, I have taken your time," he said.

The silver-gray topcoat disappeared in the shadows of the cherry trees. The sound of his footsteps on the gravel walk receded into the distance.

Some time after this, in February of 1928, I left the house one night to go to a pre-election meeting of the Farmer-Labor Party. Western dress was conspicuous, and since I did not want to be noticed I put on Japanese garments which I had not worn for a long time. Instead of going toward the main street, I turned to the dark alley, slid past the lighted window of a candy store, and hurried to the elementary school where the meeting was to be held.

The approaching election was the first since the

173

passage of general manhood suffrage, and final pre-election meetings were being held here and there. Up to this time, platforms had seldom been announced, even at the approach of general elections. Instead, vote-getters in groups of two or three had come to our *genkan* numberless times during the pre-election days. They wore their *hakama* and black haori with their household crests, and almost prostrating themeselves on the ground, they pled for "one pure vote" for their candidate. They held the ceremonial white fan in their right hands, and the fans, opened an inch with thumb and forefinger, clicked *patchi-patchi.* Also in the old days numerous rolls of letters endorsing the candidates arrived and were placed before Father each morning. They were written in black ink on fine heavy *hōsho* paper, but Father always threw them into the wastepaper basket without even bothering to open them. It seemed to me when I was small a shame to throw them away.

Recalling such things about elections in former days, I reached the elementary school. The building, usually sunk in darkness, was alive with brilliant electric light. On the paneled wall of the gymnasium were pasted narrow strips of paper with big characters in ink. I began reading, from right to left, such slogans as, "Limitation of armaments and establishment of world peace"; "Oppose sending army to meddle in China"; "Eight-hour workday." I could read no more, because the strips were hidden by the backs of policemen who had come to the meeting.

There were no chairs in the gymnasium; a thin

174

straw mat with curled and raveled edges was spread on the bare floor. I stood at the entrance and waited in line as the police inspected one by one the people who were coming to the meeting. I noticed that before sitting on the mat everyone took off his geta and wrapped them in newspapers brought from home. About two-thirds of the mat was filled up with people, rubbing against each other's shoulders, carefully holding on their knees their geta bundles. Sitting there they leaned forward a little, as if they were putting all their strength into their bodies. Not many of them were dressed in Western clothes; many wore dark, simple cotton with hardly perceptible stripes.

I thought I heard someone calling my name behind me. Looking back, I saw the intelligence officer who had come to call on me, standing and smiling slyly. Since that day, whenever I met him by chance on the street he had stopped and talked familiarly to me, as if we were old acquaintances. My heart pounded at meeting him in such a place, and I felt as though I had a water brash. As I pretended calmness so that he would not be able to see into my mind, he beckoned me to a place somewhat removed from the groups of people. Drawing his eyebrows up to a peak and staring at me, he urged me to go home.

"If you go quietly," he said, "there will be no difficulty later." I felt the threat in his words.

I left the meeting and, gazing up at the coldly-cleared starry sky, silently I retraced my steps homeward.

Detention Cell

A LITTLE MORE than a year after this experience at the Farmer-Labor Party meeting, I was in the garden one Sunday afternoon. Father and Younger Brother had gone for a walk. My two half-sisters, who had returned home after a long stay with their grandmother, were with me. We were busy grooming the garden in which the azalea flowers had just begun to bloom, when a maid ran out excitedly. In a choking voice she told me that someone from the police station had come to see me.

In order not to frighten my half-sisters, I went quickly, just as I was, through the garden and around to the *genkan*. An intelligence officer, wearing a Western suit, was staring at the surroundings. When he saw me, he said in a tone of command, "These matters cannot be discussed here. Come outside a moment, please."

I thought the request was strange, but I was less

concerned with its strangeness than with the impossibility of going outside in my indoor clothing. I said, "Please wait a moment." But as I stepped away, the officer suddenly seized my sleeve and held it.

"That costume will be all right," he said.

Just then I caught a glimpse of the navy blue uniforms of policemen behind the cherry tree by the gate. My heart thumped as though it had bumped against something. This situation was very grave. I felt as if my blood were sucked down through my body and might flow out from the tips of my toes.

I went out to the gate, the intelligence officer close behind me. A Ford car, with doors open, was standing there. The street was so quiet, there was not even the shadow of a passer-by. I got into the car and it tore down the street, jolting me with its motion. Where was I being taken? For what reason? These thoughts whirled like a fire-wheel in my mind. I closed my eyes, trying to regain calm. But the lurching of the car shook my mind. "Even this? Even this?" it seemed to say accusingly. I felt that I was being dragged into some domain whose boundaries I did not know. Whither? Why? When I thought the car had been running twenty or thirty minutes, it stopped, stopping the thoughts in my mind. In front of me was a frame building. Peeling paint exposed its dirty, sooty boards. Policemen were hurrying in and out. I knew it was a police station.

In a room near the entrance, three or four policemen sat at desks and turned over documents. I went through this room and into a dusky, moldy-smelling corridor. There was a policeman on either side of me. The sound of their sabers beat into my brain. At the end of the long corridor was a large, thick, iron door. One of the policemen slid close to the door and opened a small peep-window in the upper part of it. Almost sticking his neck through the window, he said, "Please take care of one person."

His voice to me was far away, like a voice in a dream. A sound of metal scraped my mind as the door opened. My body was sucked inside; and behind me, with violent noise that ground my mind to powder, the door closed firmly. With that sound, the hope lurking somewhere inside me, beseeching freakish good fortune, was cut off altogether. Even in the car, even after I arrived at the police station, I had looked for a miracle to snatch me from the brink of evil. Now all hope was lost with the closing of the door. I thought it would never open again.

At the end of the detention room in which I was standing were three cells in a row. The metal locks of their doors glittered coldly in the semi-obscurity. In the upper part of each door was a small window, black as a cave. Something was shining in the blackness. As I looked fixedly I realized that there were people in the cells, surveying me, a newcomer to prison; the gleams I saw came from three pairs of eyes burning and shining in the darkness. An expressionless jailor stood in front of a desk at the left-hand side of the room. I was commanded to stand in front of him and to remove my belongings—a wrist watch, two handkerchiefs, twelve or thirteen hairpins, an obi

178

clasp, a waist band—which he placed on the desk, one by one, in a row. Anything that might possibly be used for hanging myself was taken away. I was told, too, to take off my geta and to put on thin, cold sandals. The jailor scrambled my things together in a soiled gray cotton bag stamped with a number 16.

The cells facing me as I came in were the ones for men. On the left were the protective rooms for women. As I stepped into a protective room, its door closed behind me with a sound that seemed to imprison me forever. It was so dark in this two-mat room that I could see nothing. I felt as though I had been put into the cold dampness of the bottom of a deep box. I sat down and leaned against the wall. My knees seemed to be breaking. Chilling coldness went through my body, freezing even my mind. Courage crumbled inside me, and I was swept with heart-paining loneliness, and anxiety, and a rising tide of fear. I felt like a small boat, dizzily spun in a whirlpool. I closed my eyes and held my head.

Someone whispered in my ear, "What were you taken in for? Stealing?"

I raised my eyes and saw a middle-aged woman with sunken cheeks peering into my face. I sobbed, overcome with self-pity.

The woman said, "When you come to a place like this, you've got to be brave." Then she was silent.

After a long while a police saber sounded *gacha-gacha*, and a hole in the bottom of the door was opened. A large hand reached in and set down two wooden boxes. They were police station lunch boxes,

179

with reddish black paint peeling off and exposing the grain of the wood. A rancid odor whiffed into my nostrils as I lifted one of the covers. Leftover food from restaurant and hospital lay dismally in the box, in a colorless, shapeless jumble. The well-lighted dining room at home flashed into my mind. The supper which had always seemed commonplace now seemed supremely delightful and consecrated. Now everyone must be worrying about me, waiting forlornly. My chest filled to overflowing, and I felt suffocated.

After the bustle of supper, a heavy stillness fell on the prison's cave-darkness. The very atmosphere seemed to weigh down my body. My cell mate began to recount little by little the story of her life. Death had taken her husband, and she had made a living for her four children by knitting jerseys at home; then her children fell ill, and, being unable to meet expenses, she had stolen a watch and ring. "My luck was bad, I can tell you," she said, and sighed.

Even though it was the end of March and spring had begun, the nights were cool. The blankets which had been given to me were small and torn; two or three were needed to cover the body; and they were sticky with dirt and grease. I had left mine at my feet because I disliked putting their damp grime against my skin; but gradually, as the cold increased, I wrapped them about my hips. The woman took one of her own and placed it upon me. "Never mind," she said, "I'm used to this kind of existence. Even if it gets cold, I'm used to it."

The protective room was just large enough for the
180

two of us to stretch out our arms and legs and lie down. In the men's cells there were not even mats, only the wooden floor; and five or six people were always crowded into them, so their feet and heads bumped into the walls and they could not even stretch out.

With eyes open wide in the darkness, I thought about home. Father's face came stealing into my mind, moving me deeply. The woman beside me snored lightly as she slept. The footsteps of the jailor going back and forth in the corridor sounded *kotsu-kotsu*, like knocking on a door. My chest heaved and I held it down, down, knowing that I could not hold it down much longer. I was thinking that the jailor's footsteps sounded less frequently, when I was startled by a scream. It continued and grew thin, then rose again in a long wail. There was silence for a while, broken by another throat-splitting cry. My heart throbbed as though it were beating a tocsin. That screaming voice did not sound like a man's voice. It was high-pitched. Was it a woman's? Now the sound of sobbing leaked through the silence between screams. I lay listening, and heard a noise like that of a body being beaten with something. I sat upright, without thinking, and shook the sleeping form of the woman. She told me that a thirteen-year-old boy was being tortured; he had worked in a brewery and was suspected of stealing from his master, but he refused to confess.

Toward dawn, just as I was dozing, I was awakened by a yell from the jailor. I was dazed and dizzy from

181

lack of sleep. I could do nothing but sit still as time passed by. I could only live through the minutes one by one. High on the wall was one window, about a foot square. Through this window, between iron bars, I caught a glimpse of blue sky. On the sooty walls around me fingernails had carved out characters, but it was too dark for me to read them. In the afternoon, a child about six years old was brought into the protective room.

"Mummy," he sobbed to my cell mate, "you said you would buy rice syrup and come right home, and you told me to wait quietly, but you didn't come back!"

At that moment the door opened. The jailor called, "Number 16! Number 16!" My examination was going to be held.

I put on cold damp sandals and went down the long corridor. The noise of the sandals as I walked sounded like someone chasing me. I was taken to a room on the second floor of the prison. Around a large desk in the middle of the room four or five intelligence officers were sitting. On the wall facing me was a placard bearing the slogan, "Be kind and alert." I sat on a chair pointed to by one of the officers, and found myself in front of an officer with a Kaiser-like mustache who seemed to be the superior of the others.

He said, "To conceal will not be to your benefit." His voice was authority piled on authority. He took several letters from the top of the desk and showed them to me. They were letters which had been sent to me during the last election by Mr. Yamada, the

182

chairman of the election committee of Japan's Farmer-Labor Party. I had become acquainted with Mr. Yamada when he came as lecturer to the discussion group which met at my house; he had also contributed manuscripts to *Woman and Labor*. Probably the police had searched my home when I was brought to the prison, and had found the letters. So I learned at last that Mr. Yamada was going to be persecuted for harboring dangerous thoughts, and that I had been put in the detention cell simply because I was an acquaintance of his.

The officer wrote my explanation into the records, put down his pen, stiffly twirled his upstanding mustache, and glared at me. "Is that all you know? Then that will be all."

The next morning, after being warned against involving myself in such matters in the future, I was led out of the back exit of the detention prison.

When I went out into the street, the sunlight was dazzling-bright. My eyes and mind blinking together, I looked back over the way I had come in the past few years. Although I had walked slowly, twisting and turning, it seemed to me that I had come forward. I felt that now I was standing at the turning point. One way was a steep mountain path strewn with rocks and roots of giant trees; the other was level, and even with eyes closed one would not stumble on it. . . .

As I looked at my surroundings, it seemed to me that trees and streets and people walking about had changed during the three days I had not seen them, that the whole world had changed altogether.

Coming to America

THE GONG stopped its agitated ringing, and the steamer which bore me slowly left Yokohama Harbor, stirring the turbid water into large waves that beat against the piers. In my hands thin strings of varicolored tape trembled, as though sending me the thoughts of those on shore. As the ship moved away the strings were pulled out longer and longer, then were cut off one by one. Some tangled tape clung to the side of the boat, like my heart wrenched and torn and pulled asunder.

The faces of those who had come to see the boat leave dimmed into a hazy mass and were sucked into the grayness of the pier. Only a yellow and a purple parasol on the end of the pier jutting into the water, caught the sunlight and soaked into my eyes forever. The sea near the harbor was heavy and thick. The wake of the boat was like a long tail, and at its tip the city of Yokohama floated like an island. The town of low-crouching tile roofs grew smaller and smaller before my gazing eyes; and I murmured, "*Sayonara, sayonara*—good-by" as the last bit of shore sank into the sea.

This was the year 1930. Four months earlier Father had left for Europe to fulfill his long desire to study abroad for three years. It was at that time that talk of my coming to America had begun. Father, leaving this same harbor, had said very briefly, "Haru, what do you mean to do about yourself?" And all of the relatives, after a conference, had decided to entrust me to my aunt and uncle who were coming to America.

For four months after Father left I lived at home with the third mother whom he had married as a duty to the family. At first he had strongly opposed marrying again, but finally relatives had persuaded him that it was necessary to have a woman to care for the family during his absence, and so it was hastily decided that he would receive the new wife. After his departure, as I looked at the figure of New Mother standing on the veranda and gazing unseeing at the garden trees, I was suddenly lonely. Looking at the back of her who had married to take care of my younger sisters and brother, who had been entrusted with affairs of the household during Father's three-year absence, who bowed meekly to her fate, I began to have a feeling of reproach toward my father. I divined the distress of the mother who had married

185

into a family of grown children, and I had the desire to speak to her as woman to woman rather than as daughter to mother. But, I asked myself, if I did that, would I not hurt New Mother's feelings? Finally I decided that in New Mother's mind was hidden the fate of resignation, and I carefully acted as daughter to mother. But I was glad to make her worry somewhat lighter by leaving for America.

To all of my relatives my departure was a relief. I was considered eccentric. It was unconventional and therefore annoying to have such a person in the family. Because I was not inclined toward a marriage through a go-between like Elder Sister's, and because I remained carefree in spite of the fact that I was about to pass the marriage period, I was incomprehensible. "It is improper," complained the aunt who was taking me to America, "when a girl like Haru, older than twenty, still remains unmarried."

Moreover, I had added one more thing to the list of my disgraceful activities by attending lectures at Waseda University. For a long time men's universities had excluded women; but recently, influenced by the world trend toward equal education for men and women, they had opened their doors a little and allowed women to attend lectures only. I was considered to have soiled the name of my family and ancestors by mingling with men students and having them as friends. Elder Sister and Oba-san were always saying, "Haru, they say that you have been seen nonchalantly walking on the street with young men students. Please consider what a reflection this is, first

186

on your father, and then on all the rest of the relatives." I felt as though both my mind and my body were shriveling when I heard these words. During my high-school days I had had these same ideas; but my present mind was far distant from their way of thinking, having departed from it, I do not know when.

Now the ship was carrying me into the open sea, where the blue ocean stretched to the horizons. The crowd of people who had surrounded me were no longer on deck. Uncle and Aunt were probably in their cabin. I alone, desolate, gazed at the sky above Yokohama. A bouquet of yellow chrysanthemums in my hands brought me the fragrance and remembrance of the shore; the large flowers bent back their heads as if to peer into my face. All feelings of affection that ever had stirred in my mind, that ever had wrapped me gently and warmed the blood in my body, rose up in love for my country. Impatient with its damp and outworn customs, I had sometimes forgotten affection; but now that I was leaving, it boiled up painfully.

That night a clear moon rose. Moonlight flowed drippingly on the black water. Out on the deck alone, I gazed at the sky. That full moon, spreading its blue-white light on my home, on the land of my memories, would also shine on the other side of the earth. It was so clear, it seemed it might reflect the thoughts of my heart and communicate them to those who were far away.

Not even the shadow of a person moved on the midnight deck. My body, all alone, seemed to float on

187

the ocean; and my mind drifted, too, on the sea that
reached from shore to shore. All my life, I thought,
had been unceasing pain. Always I had sought something the eye could not see; and always when I
touched it, it had slipped away from my fingers. My
mind, scraping against the world, had been wounded.
I cried alone in my loneliness. If I had trod the safe
path, not gazing at the great wide sky, not seeing the
far mountains which beckoned me on; if I had accepted my grandmother's world, perhaps now I would
be living a calm and peaceful life, like Elder Sister's
life, where no waves beat. But my mind, flying about
in the sky, had listened to the whispering voice of the
wind, and the rustling of leaves of the trees, and the
fine vibrations of air. What shore would I reach, being
like this, and when?

Father's parting words remained with me, bored
into my memory: "Haru, what do you mean to do
about yourself?" Sometimes it seemed to me that he
was scolding the obstinacy with which I persisted in
my own way, reproaching my wandering thus far
without arriving anywhere; it was as if he had thrown
me out and commanded, "Now manage your destiny
yourself." But again it seemed to me that Father was
worrying with me, and encouraging me who walked
all alone.

Since the time when I held in my arms the blue-
eyed doll which Father gave me, I had drawn a picture of America in my mind, and had sought it beyond
the horizon fading into evening haze. But now, when

188

I realized that I was actually going to America, I was frightened. A dream-America, peering at me from the shadow of the moon, beckoned to me, gently smiling. But the real America which, like an eagle, might grasp me and toss me about—I wondered if it would not make me dizzy.

The engine in the bottom of the boat throbbed faintly, like the beating of my heart. The clear moon peered into my soul. I remembered the poem,

> *The wave that rolls up,*
> *Rumbling on the shore*
> *Of the great sea,*
> *Breaking me,*
> *Bursts in spray, and scatters.*
> —Minamoto Sanetomo

For the ocean, sleeping under moonlight, was beating and receding in my mind, raising a high white spray.

PART FOUR

Nostalgia

SAN FRANCISCO, floating on the morning mist, drifting over the waves in a trance, was like an island in a dream. To me it looked like an island in Japan, and I gazed at the dawning sky, expecting to see the grace of snow-peaked Fuji Mountain. As the ship approached the shore, green groves, red roofs, and white windows dropped calm shadows on the surface of the water, and the illusory Fuji disappeared without leaving a trace.

Even after I had landed in San Francisco and stood on the unmoving earth, I felt the ground rocking under my feet. In the different-to-the-skin air of this strange country, my blood seemed to be running backward. Tall buildings, weaving flow of automobiles, and jarring noise of streetcars seemed to be roaring at me. Short gay dresses of red, yellow and blue

193

danced past me. Thrusting out their chests, stretching their waists, and standing as straight as green bamboos, the women walked by kicking the streets. To my eyes used to the timorous gait of Japanese women, who walked with short steps, drooping shoulders, and eyes cast down, these figures of women were a symbol of free, unhampered womanhood.

It was Labor Day, early in September. The noise of a band resounded in the crowd as a procession passed. People in the procession and policemen standing by were smiling like elementary school children on a picnic. If this had been Tokyo, the procession of workers would have been surrounded by cordons of police; the horses of mounted police would have stamped their hoofs, and the marching faces would have looked strained.

What an uneasy feeling it gives one not to be able to understand the language of a country! What language, supposed to be English, had I learned in Japan? Around my ears buzzed an incomprehensible sound, like the sound of bees whose hives have been disturbed. I strained my ears again and again, but no meaning was born out of the noise. The buzzing resounded in my head even when I stood on a calm cliff overlooking Golden Gate. The expectancy of knowing America seemed to crumble before this unfamiliarity of language, and the ringing in my ears was like the uneasy sound of the crumbling of my hope.

When Uncle and Aunt and I were inside a train crossing the American continent to Washington, I felt myself shrinking smaller and smaller. I felt like a lost

194

child thrown out into this wide country. The great boulders of the Rocky Mountains piled heavily upon me as I looked from the window of the train; the crags looked like giant fists, sometimes like arms jutting out. Even at nightfall, after the train had rushed and rushed all day, the country without even man's house or man's shadow did not come to an end; the limitless plain crouching in darkness seemed to gulp me down.

It was night when I arrived in Washington. It was much darker than I had expected; the street lights shadowed by rows of trees threw dim lights. Washington, wrapped in square flower beds and parks thickly groved, was a quieter city than Tokyo. Seeking the delicate fragrance of garden and the touch of soft earth, I wandered near a park and tried to regain my inward peace. The tumult of mind I had felt upon landing in San Francisco had not ceased to rock me. Even after my tired body was quieted, the tossing of the waves and the jarring of the train shook my mind.

Soon I began attending George Washington University. As if clinging to each word I listened to the lectures, but I did not understand the greater part of them. And when I wanted to tell new acquaintances of my feelings, I could not talk to them. Looking around the English literature class, I saw that there were more girls than men. I thought of Waseda University, where women were as rare as stars in a dark, rain-threatening sky. I remembered the eyes of men students, which had seemed to say, "What a fresh woman!" Here, if a woman dropped a pencil, a man would pick it up for her.

195

In the park I went through going to and from school, children's high-pitched voices and laughter from wide-open mouths resounded among the trees and gently brought calm to my heart. Red and blue dresses jumped about as if in a butterfly dance. A group of little girls were skipping rope. Their small white thighs received the sun and were like fish skipping over the waves, shining white and swimming in air. The autumn sky was clear and limitless, transparently blue. Over it floated white broken clouds, like white sails in the ocean, drifting in wind.

I thought of autumn in Japan: the maples in our garden turning red and scattering leaves, spread out like the small palms of a child's hand, on the surface of the pond; the bush clover by the pond, heavily drooping its wisteria-colored flowers, swaying in the wind. . . . When autumn comes the Gingko leaves drift down soundlessly about the gravestone where my mother sleeps; the yellow fan-shaped leaves lie so thickly on the black grave soil that they can hardly be swept away. . . . I could almost see my grandmother's back as she knelt before that gravestone, placing her two hands together in worship. I could hear the sound of the water bucket being pulled up, in the stilled temple garden; then the flowing sound of the clear water emptied from the bucket into a wooden pail. Grandmother, holding the pail in one hand and a thick bundle of incense sticks in the other, would visit my mother's grave. After long silent prayer she would pour the clear water over the gray gravestone, which, wet, became lustrously green. She had

made me water the grave thus when I was small, saying, "If we water it, the Buddha will feel refreshed.
. . ." Just before I left for America I had offered a
snow-white summer chrysanthemum after worshiping at Mother's grave. The chrysanthemum had stood
out in clear white relief among the deep green leaves
of the camellias that surrounded the gravestone. . . .

Sitting all alone in a park in America, listening to
children's voices, and lost in my own thoughts, I
watched the people passing by.

I yearned to discover somewhere, even in the gait
or the expressions of people passing by, one bit of
something really American. Although my body was
here, it seemed to me that America was wrapped in
mist and could not be touched. I was surrounded by
things American—the landscape, the language, the
people—but the moving American life was shut away
from me. Since I had stepped on American soil, many
shapes had reflected themselves in my eyes, but they
were shadows. I could get no glimpse into the sub-
stance of American life. I felt that I had vainly run
after figures that passed without greeting, and had
tried to cling to their sleeves. America was an unknown giant who disappeared into darkness, shaking
off my hands.

It seemed to me that I had lost myself when I
landed in this country. All knowledge and observation that were a part of me seemed to have left me,
and I felt as if I were carrying around their empty,
cast-off shells. Up to this time I had unconsciously
had a big head, thinking that I was more accom-

plished than the average woman. On the boat, as I watched Aunt fondling her children, I had felt that I, who strove to understand society, was one degree above her whose mind was completely occupied with her husband's and children's affairs. When I sat on the deck absorbed in reading a book, somewhere in my mind had lurked the desire to show off my knowledge to others. With what self-satisfied eyes had I viewed the married women on the boat who moved, not as individuals, but as shadows of their husbands, growing bigger with their husbands' positions. Now I was ashamed of myself, who, with so slight knowledge, had been so proud. Now I felt broken to pieces and kicked down into a deep gorge.

I left the park and walked, deep in thought, without destination. Vine-covered houses disappeared along my way, and crooked frame houses stood in rows, as though left there from some unknown time. Half-sunken into the ground, these foundationless houses looked dark and sooty and sick.

Day by day the autumn deepened. Dead leaves still left on the bone-like, sharp-branched tips of the trees, shook in the autumn wind. I began to stay at home more and more, because it was easier to sit alone than to appear before people. At night I sat by the window listening to the sound of dead leaves scattering in the wind. Rain began to fall on the dead leaves, making a pattering sound.

Aunt had introduced a bachelor acquaintance to me, and had urged me, without expressing it in so many words, to associate with him. I went to a play accompanied by him. As I was leaving, Aunt took away my plain overcoat and forcefully persuaded me to wear her fur one. She who in Japan had opposed my even walking with young men, accepted American customs without question. She adopted the customs of the society in which she moved as a standard, and measured right and wrong accordingly. But it was shoulder-stiffening and painful for me to sit with a person with whom I had nothing in common, and my mind was neither on the play nor on my companion. Like a sea creature that closes its shell tightly, I closed my mind and stiffened my body.

I could not become familiar with the Japanese who surrounded my uncle in Washington. Although I tried to distract my mind from the loneliness and distress of being cut off from American society, these people with whom Uncle and Aunt associated were also far removed from me. When I came near them, I realized more strongly than ever my loneliness; it was less distressing to be actually alone. In order not to hurt Aunt, who with kind intentions arranged engagements for me, I went out with these people. But afterwards it always seemed that something bitter remained on the tip of my tongue.

These Japanese in Washington seemed to have forgotten or forsaken the dreams and ideals of youth written down on yellowed, faded pages of old diaries. Even their delicate feelings were now threadbare. They were concerned only with safe-guarding their positions. As I watched these men associating with each other, I noticed that they could not discard the cloak of position even when they were playing bridge or mah jong. When they talked with their superiors, they would bend their waists and bow at each word. The higher the companion's position, the lower their bows. When they faced inferiors, on the other hand, they dealt with them by thrusting their chests forward and pushing out their chins. Twenty such persons in a room would act thus: discriminately bowing or thrusting out their chests, to right and to left, the highest and the lowest, one to the other.

Struggling alone in the deep mud-bottom of this stagnant marsh, I wanted to go out to the wide sea, even if to be buffeted by big waves and carried away by violently breaking surf. Often in these days I remembered the lines:

> *If asked*
> *What is most painful,*
> *Answer*
> *It is the mind*
> *Sundered from other minds.*
> —Abbott Ryokan

New York City in Snow

THE DAY I CAME to New York City, a leaden winter sky hung low. At the Y.W.C.A. on Seventeenth Street I sat lonesomely in a small room, facing my few pieces of luggage. It apeared that all the women who lived in the building worked during the day; in the corridor outside the door there was no sound of footsteps, no sound of anyone moving in the rooms separated from mine by only a thin wall.

I pulled close to my knees the suitcase that had followed my body all the way from Japan. Even though it was silent, it was my only companion. The slight stains on it made me feel that my own life had seeped into it, and I stared at it fixedly. Then I opened it, took out a photograph of my mother, and placed it on a small desk near the window. From an oblong Paulownia box I lifted a *Kyoto* doll with white face,

201

crescent-shaped eyebrows, and long slit eyes. Grandmother had given it to me as a parting gift, saying,
"Even if you go to America, don't forget to come back
to Japan." The doll stood on the desk, showing beneath her scarlet undergarment a row of small white
toes.

Outside the window, powdered snow, dancing like
mist, fell from the ashen-colored sky. Neither Mother's
photograph nor the *Kyoto* doll in front of the fogged
window pane could warm me. I shuddered with
cold. The jarring noise of the elevated train that ran
near by broke through the soundlessly falling snow,
scratching and tearing and shaking the air. As I
watched, white snow kept piling up on roofs and
streets. Pressing my cheek against the cold window
pane and looking down at streets buried in whiteness,
I thought of the Washington I had left.

To Aunt, my idea of coming to New York alone had
been wild and foolhardy. "When at last it's been arranged that a maid will come from Japan!" she said.
"I was just thinking that from now on we two could
be entirely carefree, and buy clothes and sew the kind
of suits we like, consulting with each other about
materials and patterns."

To this I was silent, looking down, and she said
half-teasingly, "Haru is really a whimsical person,
isn't she? Purposely trying to experience hardships!"

She had laughed, and had not taken me seriously in
the beginning. But when she knew my unexpectedly
determined mind, she anxiously consulted Uncle, and
then told me that she could not let me go to New York

without my father's permission. "As long as you are entrusted to us," she said, "we have a responsibility, and we cannot let you do as you please without your father's consent."

Before long a letter came from Father, who was in Germany, absolutely opposing my plan, as Aunt had anticipated. I myself had not expected Father's permission to leave Washington. But by this time I had determined to live my life as I thought fit, disregarding even Father's wishes and worries. Various thoughts were beating wildly in my brain. The atmosphere of Washington was unbearable to me. Just as a stream flowing among mountains will, if checked, break its dam and suddenly overflow, so I, whose outlet of expression was obstructed, sought a way of escape.

My uncle had tried to stop me by speaking of the terrors of New York. "Subways stretch and wind about like spider webs," he said, "and once you get underground you won't know where you're being carried to. Then too, on the Broadway that rivals daylight, holdups are rampant." In Uncle's eyes I was no more than a small girl who could be frightened by such bugbears.

The white snowflakes dancing at the window were sucked away into the twilight of the shorter winter day. The dusk seemed to threaten my body, as if it would whirl me into it. I felt myself falling into the deep bottom of growing darkness. Only the white face of the *Kyoto* doll on the desk remained visible. In the windows of houses facing me, the lights began to glow. I could see them warmly enfolding families at their peaceful evening meals. Once again I thought of Washington. Aunt's face, floating palely out of the darkness, seemed to whisper, "All would have been well if you had stayed with me."

The scene of a ball to which Aunt had taken me came to my mind. The crowd dancing under pale lights had looked like the swelling of waves that quietly come and go under moonlight. Dazedly I had listened to the dance music, which made me wonder if it were the sound of strong wind among pine trees. For nearly a week after the ball, bouquets for me had been sent to Uncle's office from a person said to be the son of a minister from a small European country. Not knowing that Uncle was a relative of mine, he had asked him to search for me, saying, "She was a Japanese lady." Uncle only laughed and did not bring the bouquets home; he said that he told the man he did not know any girl of that description. I had not even asked what kind of flowers they were. If I had gone about with Aunt, looking at ladies' dresses which all looked equally beautiful to me, attending the theater with her, enjoying the social gatherings to which she went, I would not have had to taste this loneliness which was tearing out my heart. If I had been able not to think, to keep my mind empty, life in Washington would have been satisfactory to me.

But it had not been so; and now, sitting alone with drooping shoulders and head cast down, I wondered if I would vanish and disappear in bottomless New York. I was like the leaf of a tree drifting in mid-ocean, shaken by rough waves, and I might even be drowned. I was like a small bird released from his cage who now sat shivering on the winter-withered branch, not at all the bird he had hoped to be. I who had been like a potted plant grown in a greenhouse, was now a wild flower exposed to cutting wind and the freezing cold of the winter storm.

I lay in bed as night deepened, hearing the jarring noise of the elevated rushing out from black darkness. And when that ended, I heard the sound of things freezing, streets and houses cracking in the cold. It stopped snowing the next day, but the wind blowing wildly over high-piled snow, stormed the whole day through. In Tokyo there were no days like this. There we had peaceful, snow-melting mornings, when the warm sun melted the soft whiteness, and shining drops of water fell drip-drip from the garden pine; when melting snow-water flowed along the eaves with a sound like a mountain stream.

I visited a Japanese pastor in uptown New York, with a letter of introduction which I had received when I left Japan. Three small sisters came out, greeting me like a playmate. As I went with them to bounce balls, I noticed for the first time in a long while the pale sunlight falling slantingly on the streets through clouds that were thick like lead.

At the pastor's home, I saw in a Japanese newspaper published in New York a piece of art criticism by a man to whom I also had an introduction. It had been given to me by an ex-professor of Waseda University, who had told me that this artist lived in Greenwich Village, and that I should meet him without fail because he had lived in New York for a long time. Seeing his article in the newspaper, I felt like searching him out the very next day. At the entrance to an elevated station I bought a small New York guidebook with a red cover.

The following day, with the map in one hand, I walked about looking for Greenwich Village. I passed sooty brick houses half-buried in the dirty snow. A man with shapeless hat pulled over his eyes went by, followed by a big-hipped old woman carrying a shopping bag, almost dragging the skirt of her black dress as she heavily walked through the slush. Walking along a narrow street where the grime of poverty drifted, I turned right. Here houses heavily fitted with lustrous doors, conspicuous even to night eyes, were visible through shrubbery and iron fences. From their large windows bright light flowed onto the plants outside. These houses seemed to be back to back with the dirty houses I had seen a moment before; but here even the air seemed clear.

Streets ran wildly and wilfully, stretched right, left and obliquely, unlike the checker-board streets of surrounding New York City. Standing on dark corners and reading the names of streets, I kept on walking without direction. Suddenly it was bright ahead of me. Two or three cabarets, painted garish red, yellow and green, ran out onto the gay street. In front of them, doormen dressed as pirates and bullfighters were calling customers. I passed an antique store, a shop displaying necklaces and rings, some basement

206

tearooms, and again entered a section of dark cellars. Under the elevated of Greenwich Street the shadows of the iron pillars stretched long, looking as if brawny arms might be thrust out from behind them. At that corner, the sign "Horatio Street" hung dimly in the light. It was the street I was looking for. I walked down it past unlighted houses for nearly a block and a half before I came to number 73.

The outer door when I opened it made a loud creaking noise, as if the whole house would break down. I found the artist's studio at the very top of the dark stairs. It was unexpectedly bright and tidy. An easel stood a little toward the right in the large room, and the walls were covered with paintings—so many that there was little space between them.

"You're awfully late," I was told. And when I looked at my watch, I saw that it was nearly two hours after the time agreed on over the telephone. When I told how I had lost my way, and how ominous it was under the elevated, the artist said that this section had formerly been a slum nest, and that even taxis sometimes lost their way. He talked about the pranks of the neighborhood children when he had first moved into the section. When the slum tenements had been renovated, he told me, and artists, teachers and writers had moved in, the people living there had been hostile toward newcomers different from themselves. This was probably because rents were raised and they were chased out. The children had thrown stones and snowballs and played other pranks. On the day he came, snowballs as hard as rocks broke through the new window panes and bounded into the room. When he went outside, some ten neighborhood children, all dressed in rags, all from six to ten years old, ran toward the corner like sparrows. Realizing that he was not very angry, they took a fighting position and advanced on him slowly, packing snowballs with quick hands. One of them who appeared to be a sort of captain shouted, "Look out! He has his hands in his pockets!" So he stretched out both hands and showed them his empty palms. Seeming relieved, the children threw away the snowballs and approached slowly. He beckoned them to come into his room. They shuffled in and looked curiously at his pictures. But when they noticed the telephone, they looked up with suspicious eyes, as if they were saying, "Has he called the police station?" A quick-eyed child was stationed at the entrance to watch for the police. Meanwhile the artist gave the other children bananas which he had bought cheaply, and began to sketch their faces. They thrust their dirty faces up one after another, saying, "Me too, me too." They did not mind whether the pictures looked like them or not. Holding them with great care, they rushed out, kicking the floor with their torn shoes. From that time on they did not break windows. Whenever they saw a Japanese face around the corner, they rang his doorbell and announced, "A guest is coming." Once a child was sent by its mother to give him a clay Japanese doll.

This man's story indicated that he was used to the life of the slum streets. Although he had come to America when he was a child, and had been here for twenty years, he still read Japanese newspapers and magazines, and was well informed on Japanese affairs. For the first time since I had left Japan, I found a companion with whom I could talk. And although this was the first time I had seen him, I stayed for a long time.

Late that night he accompanied me home. A Japanese man walking on the street with a woman leaves her behind, even when crossing the street, and goes ahead unconcernedly by himself. But this man walked with me, by my side. I felt that he was a cross between American and Japanese. Fourteenth Street, frozen and hard, shone under the lights as if it were wet, and stretched straight toward the far distance.

Love with Anger

ABOUT A YEAR after I came to New York, Father, who was in Europe, decided he would return to Japan by way of America. During this year I had been living in the home of an American pastor helping his wife in her housework and managing to attend lectures at Columbia University.

Nearly three years had passed since I had parted from Father in Japan, and now, waiting impatiently to see him, I searched my memory for his features. Strangely enough, when I tried to recall the whole of his face, the outlines which had seemed so clear dimmed and vanished into air. But his eyes and the sides of his mouth as he began to smile, floated into my mind.

Because of storm, Father arrived in New York a day behind schedule. The blizzard of the previous day was over, and the light-dulled winter sun fell life-lessly on frozen streets. In the building at the pier, the sound of luggage trucks and footsteps rose to the high ceiling and whirled around, reverberating against the four walls. I did not know about getting a permit to go beyond the railing, so I was stopped at the gate, and I waited there for Father to come.

I saw him in the distance, tossed by waves of men, and I signaled him by waving my hands. He peered here and there, not even looking toward me, as he was pushed along by the people. He was wearing an over-coat with fur collar which I did not remember seeing in Japan. In his right hand he carried a large white cardboard box, holding it as though it were a precious thing. Surely, I thought, he must see my face as he approached me, for I was leaning far over the railing. But he only stared at me through his spectacles with a strange expression, gathering frowns on his fore-head.

"Father!"

"Oh, then, it is you, isn't it, Haru?"

He had not recognized me, and he laughed and joked, saying that I did not look like a Japanese, but like an American. There were more gray hairs in his mustache, but three years of life abroad, free from household cares, had made his mind younger; and he affected admiration for everything, saying that New York women were all beautiful. The box he was carry-ing held a toy brought from Germany for Uncle's son in Washington. He was afraid it would be broken if he gave it to a porter to carry.

All the time I was sightseeing with Father in New York, I was wondering if he would speak about my having left Washington without his permission, but he did not touch on it. One day he, who had never before paid any attention to clothes, noticed a woman's coat displayed in a Fifth Avenue shop window. "That kind of coat might look well on you, Haru," he said, looking at me, "and it would be much warmer than the one you have on." He bought me a new coat.

After some ten days of sightseeing in New York, I went to Washington with Father. Fresh from the crowds of New York, I thought that Washington, wrapped in groves, was as quietly stilled as if all motion had stopped; even the rhythmic footsteps on the street were leisurely and reposeful. The I who had first arrived in Washington from Japan and the I of today were so different—it was no wonder Father had mistaken me at the pier. The one year of living among strangers in New York, unprotected by Father's name and position, had strengthened me. The cold-blowing wind of the world had deepened my mind.

There had been great change in Japan's international relations in this year I had been away from Washington. Japan, after following a peaceful diplomatic policy for ten years, had been dragged by the Army into the invasion of Manchuria. The Manchurian incident had been succeeded by the Shanghai incident; and, having violated international treaties, Japan announced her withdrawal from the League of Nations. I was beginning to view these events with clear eyes.

In the park in Washington which I had passed on my way to school, children were playing as usual, jumping about with red cheeks in the cold wind. The trees on the streets stretched their dead branches into the winter sky as they had a year before; but now I possessed within me a strength and confidence which I had not had then.

In the train on the way to Washington I had at last confessed to Father the things I had wanted to tell him. I told him that I had met the man whom I wanted to marry; that he was the artist whom Father had met in New York; that he and I had congenial ideas and tastes. Father listened, only nodding, speaking no word of consent or admonition. After we arrived in Washington, I waited for him to speak, but he did not. I could not change my path, whatever he said, but I hoped for his permission.

When I thought about love, I realized that I had experienced the feeling for the first time when I was very small. In fifth grade in elementary school there had been a young man teacher who read to us the works of famous writers. Admiring them, he would say, "This part shines." I loved him secretly, and when he praised my compositions I felt a face-blushing, bashful happiness. I imagined that he lived in a house with a beautiful flower garden, and I longed to visit it sometime. But when Aunt took me to his house after I had finished elementary school, to thank him for his care during that time, I saw him come nervously out of his shabby, wretched house, in a cotton short-sleeved kimono. My dream was shattered all at once,

213

and instead of a fairy-tale king, a poverty-stricken figure remained in my lonesome mind. In Girls' High School I was taught that it was a sin to fall in love, and even the form of pale, childish love dissolved within me. At the time of Elder Sister's marriage and afterward, I had feared marriage, realizing that a married woman must give up her freedom and her hopes. Now I thought how I had changed since that time; and I tried to understand the change in myself in order to understand Father's thoughts about my marriage.

One day after supper I was called formally before Father, Uncle and Aunt. Although my mind was made up, when I saw their unsmiling faces I was struck by the heavy atmosphere; my body became stiff, my head fell involuntarily, and my eyes looked down at my feet. Father, Uncle and Aunt remained silent for a long time, each waiting for the other to open his lips first. Glimpsingly I looked at Father. He was deep in thought, his right hand under his chin, his face bowed down.

Aunt opened her mouth, saying in a strange, stiff voice that marriage based upon love was bestial. "I cannot agree," she said, "to a marriage that lays emphasis on love, on coming together when you like each other and wilfully separating when you dislike each other. On top of that, the other party, I hear, is an artist, so there is more ground for objection. You think you are wise, Haru, but you don't have experience of the world." To Aunt, all artists were licentious and drunken and went about seducing women with sweet words.

Uncle, folding his arms as though deep in thought, said, "Artist and poverty go together. If he had position or fortune, there would be room for consideration."

Father, wearing an expression that seemed to say this had become a troublesome affair, kept silent.

"What kind of feeling did you have when you met this artist in New York?" Aunt asked Father, turning toward him and speaking as though artists were a separate species of mankind.

"I didn't get an especially different impression. . . ." Father twisted his mustache. This was a habit of his when he was displeased.

It was decided at this conference that Father would take me back to Japan. But I was determined to go through with my plan, and I resisted Father coldly. Even though he said he would take me to Japan, he could not drag me away by force with a rope. Love between father and daughter changed to anger, and love and anger vied with each other in our hearts. After a few unpleasant days, I decided to leave Washington.

On the day I was to leave, with a promise not to see the man even after my return to New York, Father went out listlessly in the morning, saying that he was going for a walk. He had not returned in the afternoon when the time came for my departure. I returned to New York without a parting word, embracing the last view of Father disappearing among the trees on the street. At that time I could not foresee the future;

even today I do not know what day I shall again meet my father with whom I parted thus.

Winter left, spring passed, summer's heat changed to the season of coloring leaves; and one day in autumn, when clear sunlight dropped clean-cut shadows on the ground, my uncle came from Washington to New York and conveyed to me a message from Father permitting my marriage. Uncle, in Father's place, met the partners of the marriage. No words of felicitation, no gifts such as Elder Sister had received, came from my relatives. Only a letter from Father reached my husband. In it was written: "Although Haru is inordinately self-willed and inadequate, I would ask you to look after her in the long future."

In Father's eyes I was imprudent and uncontrollable, a self-willed daughter who chose her own way regardless of a parent's advice. I could see how he must feel when he compared me to Elder Sister, who had known how to guard herself, who had said that she would marry no one but an Imperial University graduate. I understood, for the first time, Father's anger which took so long to melt.

The Falling of New Sprouts

MY DEAD BABY had seemed to lie in a motionless, innocent sleep. It had been small but fully developed, its fingers and toes separate and beautiful. The features of that child who had been born before full moons and had made its journey from darkness into darkness, remained forever in my eyes. Now, remembering the sorrows of that time, I tried with all my body to protect the new life sprouting within me. It seemed to me that the small soul which had been lost had been transferred to the child now to be born, that the lost child was to be resurrected.

But the sorrows of the death of my first baby attacked me in dreams, and I had the illusion that the second life, whose motion I faintly felt, was also cut off from my life. Awakened by such nightmares in the dead of night, I lay with stiffened hands and legs, and,

217

half doubting, half believing, stared into the thick darkness.

Many friendships poured in upon me during this painful time. It was arranged that a first-rate special-ist, far beyond our means, should take care of me. I received much kindness and attention. When summer came, we avoided the heat and stayed in the home of a kind friend who lived in the country. Sitting in the shade of trees, I watched the light of leaves rustling in the sun, or gazed up at the shining silver-gray sum-mer clouds floating in the sky; or I walked along the shore of the lake. The lake reflected the trees in its green water, and from its deeper bottom the reflected sky peered out.

Spending such peaceful days, I waited for the day of childbirth, counting the days one by one; and I could think of nothing but that. Soft cheeks of a baby, limbs waving and moving incessantly, lips smelling of milk—these spread over my world, pushing all other thoughts into one corner. Could a small thing grow-ing inside me change me to such an extent? It was so. I forgot the existence of the world, and lived only for the child that was to be born.

The sacrificing love of a mother who jumps unhesi-tatingly into fire or water for the sake of her child had begun to grow within me. Once, looking at young mothers happily fondling their babies and talking silly talk, I had thought them comical. I had wondered how it could be that a mother would sacrifice her own desires and freedom, everything, for her child. Now I reflected that I too was one of these mothers. I found

218

myself from time to time almost completely egoistic from naked maternal love, and I felt frightened.

It was a hot day toward the end of August. Even in the shade of trees, stifling sultry heat wrapped my body, suffocating me. I had experienced extraordinary physical suffering, and, secretly fearing that I might again lose the child, I had given myself all possible care. Now on this day, I thought that it would be only two more months, and at the thought I felt eased, like a mountain traveler who has just crossed a steep pass and has come to an easy down-hill path. But on this very day I had to be rushed suddenly to the hospital. Going from the country to New York, still hoping for a last miracle, I made vain efforts to keep the car's shaking from being transmitted to the inside of my body.

When I had been in the hospital before, I had been surrounded by fortunate mothers lying in rows to right and left of me, proudly holding their babies to distended breasts while I covered my face to conceal my tears. For a moment I had hated these mothers who held round healthy babies. I had tried to put down such an ugly emotion, and, tightly grasping my shameful self, had stared at the walls and ceilings of the ward, trying not to see the mothers and babies lying next to me. As if understanding the anguish I had known then, my friend, who was the mother of two children, put me this time into the best private room in the hospital. "Don't worry about money," she said when I protested. "All of us together can do something about it."

The baby who saw the light of the world two months too soon was small and weak, but a beautiful girl child. She did not cry right away after birth, and I, half in dream, cried out, "She is dead! She is dead!" After a while, when my hearing was clearer, I heard the faintly audible birth cry. Then I felt I must weep with joy, thinking, "Ah, it has designed to live!"

I spent the whole night without sleeping, feeling somehow that the baby might cease to breathe if I closed my eyes. The pediatrician guarded closely the little fire of life, as if he were stirring up dying charcoal. Sometimes, in the days that followed, it looked as though it would burn, raising up a burst of red flames; then again it became like gray smouldering coal. Three days after birth, the little life, still fighting the harsh air of the outside world and almost burning out, was placed in an incubator, where it continued to last precariously. My husband visited the incubator daily, and would tell me that the baby's small hands were exact replicas of mine, or that her face was small and pretty with well-shaped eyes and nose. I did not know that during this time the child's death was considered near, and that my husband's blood was being taken for a transfusion. I could not have entertained the thought had I known. I felt that the child's life was enfolded by my mind, and that if I even imagined her death, then the thin flow of her life would cease. I lashed my mind, and desperately clung to the conviction that the child must live. I was like a mother who all alone keeps on thinking that her lost and missing child is alive somewhere, when all others believe him dead.

The baby improved to such an extent that a blood transfusion was no longer necessary. Embracing the happy hope that all would be well, I left the hospital and returned home, leaving the child in the incubator.

On that day I recalled a letter from my husband's mother. In it she said that since this was an evil year, she had gone to worship at the shrine for the purpose of casting out evil. My husband, who had left his mother when he was still a child, always wore next to his body a small amulet in red brocade case, which she had given him when he left Japan. He guarded it, not through superstition, but because he felt his mother's spirit within it. I somehow felt, too, that his mother, worshiping at the shrine to ward off evil, was guarding my child.

Weary with relief and the fatiguing events of the day, I fell into a drowsy sleep toward twilight. It was in the sleep-settled darkness of deep night that the door was violently shaken with an unusual knocking. I woke up, startled. The sound was ominous, like knocking at death's door, and at once everything was clear to me. I needed no information. All my body's blood stopped flowing.

My husband got up and went to the door. It was a messenger from the hospital. He said, "It was eleven forty-five." That voice pierced through my ears. My feet, hands and heart were paralyzed. I could not move. From my choked throat not even a groan came, only my tears flowed without check.

The short life of ten days, like a morning glory withering before strong sunlight, had been sucked away into great Nature. I could see the small child continuing her travel in the world of death, all alone. A thin path stretched without end through a boundless desert wilderness. It was neither night nor day, and a pale greenish light shone over everything. On that thin path my child dragged her feet heavily, step by step, drawing a dot of shadow behind her. I wanted to call that pitiable form and run after her. Why could I not exchange my life for the child's? Why had fate, leaving me alone, taken away the life of the child just born? So I thought and thought endlessly, and was lost in the world, not knowing what to do.

In darkness as well as in bright daylight, the lost soul of the child floated about me. The sound of falling rain and the noise of wind were like her wailing voice. It seemed to me that spiteful fate, seeing me in agony and despair, shrieked at me with cackling laughter. All the sorrow of the world seemed to lie upon my shoulders alone, to bear me down and crush me.

My sorrow, compared to the misfortunes and tragedies which many mothers bear, was insignificant. This I realized as time went on. The powers of human care and of modern science had been exhausted, so that I did not have the sadness of regretting that such-and-such a method had not been used to save the child. And the death of a baby prematurely born was a far lighter sorrow than the death of a grown child,

222

brought up in suffering. I was weak and fragile to be crushed by such small misfortune.

I remembered the words of a farmer's wife whom I had met in the province of Shinshu before I left Japan. In a low voice she had said, "To say what is hard— I felt it most when my child died." This woman, waving her wrinkled hands, had urged me to have tea. Her family of four children sometimes ate and sometimes did not. The last nursling was placed in a straw basket and left all alone, with wet diapers, near the rice field where his mother worked all day. When she came home at dusk, the empty-stomached children, tired of crying, sprawled like bundles of rags in the corners of the kitchen. The woman was sunburned, and her face was brown and thick-skinned like a chestnut. She seemed somewhere to have left behind and forgotten both joy and sorrow, as she carried so many children about in the midst of poverty. And yet she said that her child's death was the hardest thing to bear.

At that time, her feeling had been incomprehensible to me. But now her words beat against my brain. I knew for the first time the mind of the mother who lives in poverty, unable to care adequately for her children.

I had not understood this mother who worked busily with the rice plants in the fields, leaving her baby smelling of diaper in the grass near the field, putting it in the small basket as though pushing it in. When she had wanted to divide one pot of rice among her hungry children, not eating any herself, and had found the pot empty, and had loudly scolded the children, "You do nothing but eat, you bunch of grain-crushers!"—I had not understood her. I had not known the pain of a mother who cries in her heart, wishing she could feed her children until their stomachs were full, even while she scolds them with her words. Now I understood all this.

Wherever one goes there are mothers in the midst of cold and hunger, worrying about their children, restraining their bitter tears. My sorrowful tears at last spread out into a love which enfolded the mothers of the world.

> *Of the wind*
> *That has scattered the cherry blossoms*
> *The only thing that remains*
> *Is the rippling wave*
> *In the waterless sky.*
>
> —Kino Tsurayuki

Whither Immigrants

RECEIVING the bright California sun, the fresh green leaves of the palm trees, showing white bellies, swam in the high sky and dropped purple-blue shadows on the ground. Pleasant brightness seemed to enter and fill my chest.

It was the spring of 1937, and I had come to visit Los Angeles, planning to stay about six months. Of the hundred thousand Japanese said to live in America, sixty thousand are gathered around Los Angeles. For this reason, the city gave me a feeling of dear familiarity, as though I had returned to Japan, as though I had come back home after long absence.

When I went to the Japanese business section, "Little Tokyo," in downtown Los Angeles, all the air's clear brightness was absorbed in closely built rows of small gray houses, in narrow streets, and in dusty air. For an instant I felt sad; but "Little Tokyo" was filled with the fragrance and the memories of my native land, and warmly it wrapped me about.

From the chop houses with their indigo-colored drooping awnings, and from the store-fronts with their kegs of dried pickled radish and their rows of scarlet ginger, came pungently the odor of food I had eaten when I was small. It excited sensations of taste long forgotten; and, as if I had returned to childhood and again was driven by a desire to eat this and that all at once, I stood still before the eating places, inhaling the odors. The names of stores, the board signs, all the characters I saw, were in the dear familiar characters. In the small show-window of a store bearing the sign "Green Tea" in a circle, I saw teacups and tea-pots of green, semi-transparent Japanese porcelain, and black-lacquer bonbon boxes designed with golden chrysanthemums laid modestly and properly in rows. Next door to this store was a buckwheat noodle house; and behind its half-open shoji a phonograph began to play a Japanese folk song. The melancholy tune drifted into the street, bearing recollections of the native land. Inside the store, listening with absorbed, half-dazed eyes, several guests sat motionless.

The women I met on the street walked with backs rounded and faces down, taking short steps with toes pointed inward. One woman, coming out from the clothier's on the corner, stopped suddenly near me and greeted a woman coming from the opposite direction, "*Ara ma.*" Both of them, lowering both hands as far as their knees, deeply bowed and raised their heads repeatedly. It was as though hereditary Japa-

226

nese etiquette had seeped into their bodies, so that their heads dropped naturally.

At the clothier's on the corner, bright flower-patterned silk crepe, and tied and dyed waistbands dotted with red and yellow shouted out brilliant color. The beauty of soft silk overflowed the store-front, and tempted the eyes of the passing women. It was the desire of mothers to dress their small daughters, jumping about in short American dresses and showing their legs, in Japanese kimonos; to teach their daughters Japanese dancing, tea ceremony and flower arrangement; to remind them of the image of Japan.

In a vegetable store two or three houses farther down the street, a young man was sprinkling water on the vegetables. Wet spinach, brightly green and with the shining red stem-ends bundled, purple lotus roots, and pure white radishes were piled up high in rows. Even the arrangement of vegetables, unlike that in American stores, was planned skilfully and ingeniously, with a view to color. As I walked down these streets whose color, odor, voices and music reminded me of Japan, I sensed the thoughts of my compatriots in America, and I felt like exchanging words with the passing people whom I did not know.

Very soon I began to write a column for a Japanese-language daily newspaper, and every day I came to its office, which was located in the center of "Little Tokyo." Although this was America, Japanese life here was controlled by developments in Japan, four thousand miles away. Joys and worries were determined by what went on in the land of the ancestors.

Japan, since the Manchurian incident, had been more and more controlled by militarists who moved national policy at the point of the sword. In February, 1936, impaling on their swords the nation's important statesmen who refused to conform to the Army officers' ideas, they had attempted a *coup d'état*. I had heard of these incidents with sad heart. Since then, the Army had not refrained from such acts, but rather had thrust out its sword and wilfully managed the affairs of the nation.

When Japanese nations raised their voices in opposition to the Army, those voices, like an echo in the mountains, resounded unchanged in the minds of the American Japanese. The women bowing on the street, the young man in the vegetable store, the people in the restaurant listening to the Japanese folk songs, were all steadily watching Japanese society. What I felt immediately on coming to Los Angeles was the unfriendly feeling toward the Army. Worry about the land of their ancestors furrowed the brows of these people. Sometimes sighing, sometimes angry, they wanted to defend their motherland from being trampled upon and ruined by the militarists.

For my jottings-column in the Japanese newspaper I wanted to get in contact with the life of my people here, and I went hither and thither to meet many people and to listen to their sentiments and opinions. Mingling with these people taught me many things. My mind seemed to grow like spring grasses under soft rain as I touched their hearts. There are only a few Japanese in the eastern part of the United States, and I had had little occasion to know the suffering and pain of the Japanese in America. Leaving behind them the native soil where they had lived for generations, migrating to America whose language and customs were different from theirs, cutting open the path of hard living, these people had special strength to endure the suffering; and at the same time they always kept secret their solitude and their longing for the homeland.

I was staying in the home of a woman who made a humble living for her son and herself by selling cosmetics to Japanese women. She understood the people nearby as if they lay in her palms. I asked her to take me with her in her business car. Rocking over the roads with her and her cosmetic bottles, I visited the Japanese farmhouses and fishing villages near Los Angeles.

Japanese farmhouses could be recognized even from outside. The houses were small and humble; but the gardens were always thoroughly cared for, and green rows of vegetables waved in the wind. Housewives came to welcome us, rubbing their mud-soiled hands, wearing good-natured smiles on their sunburned faces. Lovable children attached themselves to the women's waists and looked up at my face curiously. When beautiful make-up creams and powders were spread out in a bare, unornamented room in a farmhouse, then the smile anticipating town-going-day shone like bright sunray on the faces of the young farm mistresses.

On Terminal Island in San Pedro Bay, which is

known as a Japanese fishing village, the men spent a twenty-four-hour day on the sea as fishermen, while the women were hired in the fish canneries. The factory whistle blew *poh! poh!*—its sound blown by a sea wind along the street smelling of fish. Japanese women in groups, three by three, and five by five, overflowed from the factory gate, kicking their white calico skirts as they trudged through the sandy dust. The fishing street, which had been bare even of human shadow, came suddenly to life, resounding with the raucous voices of the women. The houses standing in rows like match boxes on the sand were humble shanties, designed only to keep out wind and rain. When the mothers returned home, their children, who had been hiding somewhere, appeared, kicking and scattering the sand. Blue American trade-union buttons were attached to the collars of the women's white work dresses. One of the women, sitting in the entrance of her house, displayed the button proudly, saying that because of it her wages had been raised. She came from the birthplace of my husband, a small fishing village in southern Japan, and I immediately felt that there was a close bond of intimacy between us.

Seeing her smile, I felt deeply moved; for I thought that the Japanese here, even though they seem to be living on a lone island cut off from American society, are exposed, after all, to the winds and currents of the age, and are touched by them. The Japanese are treated as stepchildren by American society, and are always hedged in by fences of prejudice, but sometime, gradually, these fences may be removed. The C.I.O., from the beginning, ruled out racial discrimination and encouraged the Japanese to join; the A.F. of L., which had long refused admittance to Japanese, has also begun to take them in.

On my way home that evening, as I gazed up at the pale purple dusking sky, I thought of my husband far away. Perhaps his letter had been patiently waiting all day long on my desk. Though we were apart, our two minds were as one, and in my heart he lived always.

In the morning, while writing my column, I looked out of the window of the newspaper office upon the street of "Little Tokyo," and thought of the hidden sorrows of my compatriots. In California the notion that the Japanese are an inferior race is still prevalent. Often Japanese do not even have the liberty to rent and live in houses outside of certain districts. When they go to a barber shop or a drugstore, they are sometimes treated rudely, and even refused service. The sensitive feelings of those who live in a strange country are easily wounded by such slight things as a look or a manner of speaking. It is in order to avoid the hard, lonely feeling of having their pride trampled upon, that the Japanese cling together as closely as they do, and do not mix in American life. The street which the farm wife looks forward to visiting is not the Broadway of Los Angeles, but the minutely-built, elaborate and confusing street of "Little Tokyo." Some Japanese people grow nervous even when they walk along a street among American people, and their

231

hearts become heavy. A whole family going on a happy picnic will not choose the beautiful mountain and seashore spots which surround Los Angeles, but will go to one particular spot where Americans do not go. For fear of the treatment they might receive, some Japanese women I met had not taken one step out of the Japanese section, although they had lived in Los Angeles for over ten years.

Even though Japanese immigrants have cultivated the wild land to green, have laid down railroads and cut and brought down lumber from the mountains, and have lived several decades in this country, they cannot become American citizens. When they consider the fact that they have no right to own or even to lease the land which they have cultivated, they turn to the thought that their children, born here, will have the privileges of American citizenship, denied to them. They hang all their hopes on their children.

Most of these people who migrated to this strange land to break the new ground of their fate, were without education; and they have been so busy working, smeared with mud, that they have had no time to learn even a word of English. Whenever they gaze at their rough chapped hands, they hope their children will not suffer in the same way. It is the common desire of Japanese parents to give their children the education which will provide new vistas and opportunities in life, and often they endure great hardship in order to raise the necessary funds.

But these children in whom the parents thus rejoice gradually grow away from their elders as they ap-

232

proach maturity. It is the parents' pleasure to see the tall stature of the younger generation, and their manner of walking—lively, long-legged like the Americans'—as they go along kicking the sidewalks. But it is a grave worry to see that the children, not only in appearance, but also in manner of thinking, have become American. The eyes of the children no longer shine at the story of the Japan which the parents long for. The second generation, grown up in American atmosphere, cannot understand the Japanese customs which their parents cherish. Difference in thought between parents and children may be common in every age and in every land; but in this case, with the widely dissimilar background of Japan and America, the difference is infinitely greater.

As the second generation in Los Angeles comes of age, there are many instances where a broad, deep channel is dug between children who insist upon their independence and parents who cannot understand them. In many families, the parents speak Japanese and the children English; and the lack of a common language and the impossibility of expressing more subtle feelings, further strains the relationship. Often children who are graduated from universities find no positions open to them, and they are obliged to labor at back-breaking work like their parents—a bitter disappointment. Members of the second generation, even though they are American citizens, find themselves pushed toward social ostracism because their skin is yellow; and they tend to accept discrimination as their fate.

233

Looking down on the street of "Little Tokyo," I thought of all these things.

When summer began in "Little Tokyo," there was a gay Japanese festival. Girls, pretty in their kimonos, spread out like flowers, and, dancing to the music of the samisen, paraded all over the streets. From the eaves hung rows of *Gifu* lanterns, and wind bells tinkled in the gentle breeze. No one thought then that a month later, on the night of the Star Festival, on the seventh day of the seventh month, the Chinese incident would begin and blow a cold war wind.

In the whirl of the Sino-Japanese war, I thought sadly of my uncle, youngest brother of my mother, who had become a Chinese *Ronin*. Chinese *Ronin* carry on espionage for Japan, serving as the Army's finger tips; they enter the Chinese interior and survey the topography; or when Japan wants to start trouble, it is their duty to stir up a superficial pretext. This was the uncle who had held me steadily on his lap in the jinrikisha on the day of Mother's funeral. When I was small, he had also rejoiced and frightened me by skilfully recounting Western detective stories which he had read in translation. I remembered his face only hazily, but I still cherished a beautiful, clear, deep green jade oval which he had once brought back from China as a souvenir. I knew that he spoke Chinese well, and that he was said to look just like a Chinese when he was dressed in Chinese apparel. What was he doing now? In what part of China? My heart ached whenever I thought of him there.

234

The conflict between Japan and China began to cast dark shadows on the streets of "Little Tokyo." The Japanese watched the development of the war with troubled gaze, and prayed that it would not become serious. As at the time of the Manchurian incident, if Japan set the world against her, and relations between Japan and the United States were no longer smooth, the Japanese in America would taste the bitter cup. But the Japanese-language newspapers in Los Angeles, unconcerned with the worries and embarrassment of the people, set their pens together to justify the invasion of China. I could no longer express my opinion in the paper. Unpopular persons who had supported the Army suddenly spread out and became arrogant, their faces seeming to say, "The time has come." The serious voices opposing the war gradually diminished, as if ground to extinction. Fearing to be called betrayers of the nation, the people concealed their fears and even restrained their sighs. The atmosphere of the Japanese streets became more tense, day by day.

It was an especially hot day in the early part of September, some two months later. Even when the sun was low, the wind did not stir, and steaming heat stagnated in the narrow streets of "Little Tokyo." On the pillars at the entrance of Yamato Hall were pasted long papers bearing the characters in very black ink: "Lecture on the Truth of the Sino-Japanese Incident." Similar posters, with special vermilion circles on them, were pasted on telephone poles at strategic street corners. This was the first mass meeting since the beginning of the Sino-Japanese conflict, and the speaker was to be a Japanese Army man who had been on the scene of action in North China.

Most of the people who gathered at Yamato Hall went in hurriedly, their dark faces shining with sweat, their brows wrinkled by frowns, their expressions serious. Their bodies, which had suffered from long years of labor, were bent; their bones, thrusting out the skin, were like joints of old trees that had been exposed to wind and rain. Behind the men, the women, stiffly wearing their starched street dresses, went into the hall as if chasing their husbands. When I entered, the air was stifling with people's breathing. But the people, sitting on hard bare benches, their hands resting on their knees, listened earnestly to the story of the Army man who stood on the platform. He said:

"For the sake of eternal peace in the Orient, our Imperial Army is fighting under blazing skies against savage and merciless China. China was contemptuous of the strength of our Army, and presumptuously violated our rights and broke the peace. The Chinese population is almost drowning in the poison of Communism. Our nation, headed by the throne occupied by a single dynasty from time immemorial, was unable to bear this. In order to save our neighbor, China, we took the present step, without stint of sacrifice, and with the mercy of a parent's mind.

"Chiang Kai-shek has degenerated into a puppet of the Communist Party, and, inciting the ignorant Chinese masses, has made them resist our Army. Pitiable are the Chinese masses that are deceived by Chiang Kai-shek.

"The foreign correspondents who are on the battlefield are also deceived by the skilful propaganda of China, and are scattering false news throughout the world. Only one agency—the Domei News, which receives the news directly from our commanders—gives an authoritative and true report.

"Our nation is a superior nation, unparalleled in the world. On the day our flag of the rising sun is planted on the Chinese continent, on that day eternal peace will come.

"You who are in America have shed tears of anger and sorrow at the insulting treatment you have received. Now your fatherland is showing the world its brilliant military might. You who have such a proud fatherland can, without fear, thrust out your shoulders and walk, swinging your arms wide."

When the two-hour speech of the Army man was over, it was quickly decided, in the midst of the excitement of applause, to present an airplane to the Japanese Army, as a patriotic contribution from the Los Angeles Japanese.

My whole body was filled with a hot current of blood, and in my mind sorrow and anger ran wildly. These honest, quiet, working people were engulfed in war spirit. The anti-military, peace-loving sentiment which until recently they had held—where had it gone? For the moment they had been carried away; some day they would know and understand the truth.

Many simple people are naively moved by false

propaganda; but there are true patriots left who, though they are few in number, oppose the invasion of China fearlessly, like the pine tree which stands boldly on a steep crag. The flame in their minds will burn some day with a great light—a light which will pierce the lie-shadows that darken the earth.

A Soldier's Notebook

THE SMALL NOTEBOOK, about three by five inches, had black leather covers. The leather had been rubbed every day by the owner's hands; it had been steamed by the sweat of his body. The color had faded to a stained and spotty brown, and the worn edges and corners showed the burnt, brown underskin. Feeling that I could see in it the form of the soldier, steeped in sweat, rolling in mud, panting among bullets, I placed the faded notebook on my palm and stared at it steadily.

It was an Army notebook, one of the kind that a Japanese soldier always receives from his superior officer when he enters the Army. In it he writes every day's action. If he loses it, he is punished severely. If he dies, it returns in his stead to his wife and children. The owner of this notebook perished like dew on a battlefield in China. The notebook was preserved by the Chinese Government, acquired by an American writer traveling in China, and brought by him to New York, miles over sea and land away from the whirling fire of battle.

The touch of the cold leather seemed to seep into my hand, and in my eyes floated a long column of advancing soldiers, crawling on the ground. I could see the column of soldiers, crushed under heavy knapsacks and bayoneted rifles, dragging their feet without rest, crossing the mountains and rivers of limitless China, migrating from one gray field to another, not knowing their destination, marching with lips unmoving, and on their earth-colored faces no smile. In the heavy silence, only the confused sound of their footsteps rose incessantly from the earth. The owner of the notebook, who was one of that column and had concealed his thoughts in the notebook, seemed now to stand by my side. The notebook whispered to me in his voice.

I turned the leather cover. On the first page was written his Army address, Infantry Private in the Itagaki Division, Nagano Detachment, and his number and name. On the next page, his home address, the name of his wife, and the names and ages of his small daughters, were filled in. In the remaining space on the page, as if hurriedly added as an afterthought, were conspicuous, slanting letters in running script:

"Please be kind enough to send this notebook to my home."

The Army address and home address were written repeatedly throughout the notebook, so that his identity would still be known if the front pages were torn away.

I turned the pages, tightly filled with small characters. The record had been conscientiously written, day by day; it must have been composed word by word, earnestly, with the thought that it would go back to the loved home even if his body were buried somewhere in the grass or under the stones of China. In the early part, the letters were even, showing traces of careful brushmark. The sentences, too, strove to paint an objective picture of this soldier going to war; they were embellished with brave words like those written in newspapers. But as the diary went on, the borrowed adjectives disappeared, and honest feelings that welled up in him—fear, loneliness, uneasiness—stood naked and exposed on the pages.

I judged from the penmanship and manner of writing that this was probably a man who had had grammar school education; but there was evidence here and there that he had mastered difficult words with great effort. He was probably a man who, while working in a factory, had gone to night school and laboriously read newly published works. There are many factory workers who have persevering determination to make up for their lack of education, and who embrace knowledge with an ardor unknown among ordinary university graduates. From the notebook I drew the image of such a man. He had probably been thirty-two or thirty-three years old.

I imagined, as I read the pages, a man who, until the summons to the colors was issued, wore dusty green cotton trousers, known as rape-leaf suit, with the muscles of his arms and shoulders standing out strongly. When he returned home from the factory at night, he would carry his small daughters on both shoulders and make them shriek with joy. When the summons came, he left home and native land, parting from his old mother, his wife, and his two children. He embarked at Ujina Port on the transport *Hokushin Maru*, and when it approached the China war front, kicking the blue waves of the China Sea, his mind was deeply depressed, thinking of the family he had left behind. The moment of parting lived again in the diary:

The small, younger child, not understanding anything, was held quietly in her mother's arms. The older daughter clung to the breast of my uniform and would not let go, and she cried repeatedly, "Father, even if you go to war, don't die. Come back alive, without fail, with the Order of the Golden Eagle." That voice, that form, burn into my ears and eyes. I can never forget the image of my pitiful daughter clinging to my uniform.

On some pages of the notebook the characters were fine and sedately set down; on others, big, wild letters protruded from the lines and danced madly on the page. The characters seemed to reflect faithfully the movement of the mind:

242

Again dreamed of my wife. Even in dreams it is good. Happy to meet my dear wife.

In Kiauchau Bay many Japanese transports were floating. My mind flies to Japan. Will the day come when I will return alive in one of them, or will I become a part of the Chinese soil?

At night the truck refused to run in the mud. I walked all night over a mountain path, pushing it from behind. Tired, my body reduced to pulp.

The characters written in the trenches, while the soldier lay on his belly in mud and wrote by pale swaying candle light, were broken and wild:

It's damp and cold in the trenches. I dreamed of my wife in hardship.

In this short sentence I understood the mind of the soldier filled to overflowing with worry, and I stared at it for a long time.

On the day he went into battle for the first time, he wrote his dying wish in characters three times the usual size. His trembling mind was reflected in his trembling hand:

I think I have served my mother as much as I was able. I don't remember one quarrel with my wife who has lived with me for ten years, and I loved my children.

So it began. Then the names of intimate friends and relatives were listed, often with a broken "Good-by, good-by!", often with the repeated sentence:

243

*Thank you for all the things you did for me when
I was alive. I am dying for the nation.*

Over and over, in order to raise his depressed spirits,
he told himself that he was sacrificing his life for
the Emperor. But in the corner of this soldier's mind,
did not doubt of the need of his sacrifice reveal its
face? Did not his repetitions show his suffering and
pain?

Alive after this first battle, he continued the diary:

*Today, for the first time, received wages for fifty
days: fifteen yen and eighty sen. Kept three yen with
me and sent the rest home.*

*I wait for a letter from my wife. Wrote four-page
letter to my wife and two to my daughters.*

*When our army arrived in a small village, there
remained only old people and children for the vil-
lagers had fled. Searched the houses one by one. When
I entered one home, small children and an old mother
were sitting in fear. The children were about the same
ages as mine, and without thinking I told the old
mother that I too am father of two children of the
age of hers. Then the old mother, with a relieved
look, kindly poured out some tea for me.*

*Two Chinese captives at Lukiachwang were be-
headed again today.*

This last sentence suggests that the event was a routine one.

*In order to make our soldiers unafraid, they are
made to charge against the captives.*

244

Involuntarily I closed the notebook and dropped it from my hands. I could see the Chinese soldiers kneeling, with their hands and legs tied. I could see the up-slanting eyes, strained lips, and twisted faces of the Japanese soldiers charging with bayoneted guns. The soldiers watching the proceedings were soulless and like shells of men.

In the beginning, the charging soldiers and the watching soldiers were ordinary human beings, with gentle minds. Those minds would have been tortured in bright sunray of white day and in darkness of night by the blood-stained faces of the Chinese captives at the ends of bayonet points. But when gentleness was condemned as cowardice and femininity, when cruel violence was exalted as strength and valor, when massacre was made their duty as soldiers—then these soldiers extinguished their human minds and threw away their souls. It is said that unusually large numbers of men in the Japanese Army go insane because they are unable to bear the violence of cruelty forced upon them. Longing for the wives and children from whom they have been torn, frightened by the shadow of death and horror, they try by any means to forget their loneliness and hopelessness. They turn to wine which hardens the mind, and escape from pain into madness. The beginnings of such abnormality must have dwelt in the minds of the soldiers who watched steadily the massacre of captives.

The soldier who wrote matter-of-factly about this event was the same man who, dreaming of his wife in snatches of sleep between battles, rejoiced in that

245

brief meeting; the same man who wrote in his notebook on the twenty-eighth day of each month, "Today
is my father's death-day," and who, thinking of his
father and his son who had also died on the twenty-
eighth day of the month, dropped his head for an instant and in the trenches prayed quietly for the repose of their souls. This man was not savage. His
true image, emerging from suffering and wildness,
was that of a family's good father and kind husband.

His diary began in October, 1937, and ended February 28, of the following year. On the twenty-eighth
day, the death-day of his father and his son, he lay
flat on Chinese soil, never to rise again. I thought of
the little girl who had cried, "Father, don't die," worshiping before the family tablet which held his photograph, clasping her maple-leaf hands. I thought of
the stooped, heavy-eyed old mother, and of the wife
forlornly bearing her suffering in the winds of the
fleeting world. Their sorrows beat against my breast,
and within my heart burned hatred of the power that
started the war which destroyed this peaceful family.

The soldier who dies telling himself that it is for
the sake of the nation, the wife who tries to console
herself even a little by saying that she lost her husband for the sake of the nation—I can understand
these lonely people, clinging to this blind faith. But
do they really believe it from the bottom of their
souls? Sometimes they must wonder why and for
whom life is lost on the battlefield; the time must
come when they will know that they were deceived
in believing that it was for the sake of the nation.

Looking at the sweat-soaked army notebook, I thought with anger of the invisible forces which inexorably destroyed men who spoke my language, who were born in my country. Feeling that my heart was being gouged out and tortured, I turned the pages and read again the descriptions of massacre.

Epilogue

TODAY THERE IS a self inside me which is no longer drifting, no longer wandering, though in the past it often stumbled and many times was lost. This self has been born from the suffering and pain which I have seen on the earth, and which has rocked my heart on the traveled pathway of my life.

Before my eyes float the sweat-smeared faces of the women who pulled thick, heavy ropes to build the foundation of our house; I can hear their voices chanting, and see the babies tied on their bending backs. In recollection I trace the lifeless, dry-skinned faces of the girls in the textile factory. When I was taken to the factory from my school, my eyes looked with shallow glances at the outside forms of these girls working with sorrowful eyes in the white cotton dust and the biting noise of the machines. Today they live inside me. My heart hears their whispering voices. Their sorrows and joys are mine.

Often now I stand before audiences to speak about my country and to explain the Sino-Japanese conflict. As I speak, I hear the weeping voices of women who have lost husbands, mothers who have lost sons; I hear the painful panting breath of my people who are ashamed and heartsick and bitter because they are sent to kill and be killed in China; I hear the suppressed but ever more audible voice of my people reaching to their Chinese brothers across the sea that they shall join hands together against their common oppressors. I tell audiences that this hope is not vain; that before this war the Japanese people had voted for a liberal party and for peace; that even after the war started, many well-known men and women were imprisoned for anti-war activity; that mutinies are reported in the Army; that anti-war leaflets are found in the pockets of dead soldiers; that only the militarists have started and are waging this war. I say that America can help end it and encourage the Japanese people in their struggle for peace and freedom by a boycott of Japanese goods and by an embargo on war materials.

Driven by my desire to explain these things and to convey the longing of my people for peace, I journey for lectures—to the Northwest buried in deep snow, to dreaming New England in spring haze, to the South where red and purple soil lies under the sun. Sometimes I meet an invisible will which hides in shadows and attempts to interrupt me. But when

250

the suffering voices of my native land resound so loudly in my heart, how can I shut my ears, close my eyes, not hear them, and be silent?

I know that I have displeased my father. My New Year's card sent to him each year seems to melt away and vanish into air, and no longer brings me an answer. Even a soulless stone falling to the bottom of a valley wakens a responding echo; yet I hear only deep silence from my father, although I listen and listen, and no sound of response. I wonder with what thoughts he regards the daughter whose eyes were opened by him, whose hands were guided by his away from the narrow world of the grandmother, and whose mind has now traveled beyond his world and far away from him. I wonder on what day the thick silence lying between father and daughter will be dispersed.

I know that because of my stand it will be impossible for me to go back soon to Japan. But still I cannot be silent; I cannot betray humanity and my people. In thought, even now, I return to Japan. When I see the blue of the ocean, I am sad, remembering my country. I envy the birds of passage and in my mind fly with them over the wide Pacific. In the luminous circle of the moon I seek the reflection of my native land. When spring comes in America, I see white cherry-blossom petals drifting into the cool pool of the garden where I played as a child. My country lives in my heart.

But I am not traveling alone, searching for a dream in darkness. Around me there are many people moving in a single tide, their warm hands clasping mine. And I know the time will come when the voice of my people, like silent buds growing unseen under snow, will burst forth gloriously, in triumphant, unconquerable spring.

Afterword

THE REPUBLICATION of *Restless Wave* by the Feminist Press at the City University of New York is an event worth celebrating, for it offers new generations of readers their first introduction to Ayako Tanaka Ishigaki (1903–1996). Ishigaki's remarkable career as feminist, journalist, biographer, television personality, and activist spanned the United States, the Pacific Ocean, and the twentieth century. *Restless Wave*, originally written under the pen name Haru Matsui, is Ishigaki's only English-language book and one of the earliest of its kind by an Asian woman. It recounts in lyrical and evocative language the coming of age of a Japanese woman. Ishigaki carefully selects an assortment of stories, or episodes, taken from her own life in Japan and the United States, inviting readers to draw them together and construct from them a coherent message. The result is a text that operates on a number of levels, including prose essay, Asian American history, feminist manifesto, anti-war tract, and bildungsroman.

AYAKO ISHIGAKI'S LIFE AND WORK

Before considering various ways to interpret *Restless Wave,* it is necessary to discuss the relation of the text to its author's career and to the historical context in which she wrote. While the narrative of Haru's development in *Restless Wave* broadly follows the course of Ayako Ishigaki's own early life, *Restless Wave* is not a straightforward chronicle. Ishigaki herself referred to the book as a "novelistic semi-autobiographical text."[1] In a number of later Japanese-language writings, most notably her 1987 memoir *Waga ai no ki ni hana miteri* (I saw the flower on the tree of life),[2] Ishigaki presented a franker and more complete record of these years. The fact that the author published *Restless Wave* in Japanese translation in 1990, well after her later autobiographies had appeared, indicates that she did not consider the book as simply a first draft of her memoirs.

A comparison with her later works allows us to examine the different ways in which *Restless Wave* consciously underplays or elides aspects of the author's experience. For instance, although the real Ayako Ishigaki's upbringing resembled the life she describes in *Restless Wave,* her decision to move from Japan to the United States was more complicated than the choice she portrays Haru facing. During the mid-1920s, Ayako met and fell in love with Yutaka Aoyagi, the socially conscious son of an esteemed medical doctor. Her fiancé was hesitant to ask his father's consent to the union. Meanwhile, Ayako's sister, pregnant with her second child, asked her to accompany the family to Washington, D.C., where the sister's husband, a diplomat, was newly posted. Ayako agreed to spend a year abroad helping her sister. This would give her fiancé a chance to secure his father's consent to the marriage. However, while Ayako needed the visa she would receive as part of a diplomat's household to reside in the United States, where Japanese immigration was banned, she was more attracted by New York's progressive political and artistic reputation than by the diplomatic life in Washington. Therefore, she secretly plotted to move to New York once settled in America, and even before leaving Japan she asked around for names of contacts for jobs and housing. Among the names she received was that of the artist Eitaro Ishigaki. Ayako moved with the family to Washington in 1926, stayed until the birth of her sister's baby, and then took the opportunity to escape to New York. Using money from her father, who supported her despite his initial outrage at her actions, she audited courses at Columbia University.

Restless Wave is at its most lyrical in describing Haru's romance with the man who becomes her husband. The story behind it is no less touching. Soon after coming to New York, Ayako looked up Eitaro Ishigaki for assistance in finding work. Eitaro, ten years Ayako's senior, was an Issei (first-generation Japanese immigrant) from a poor family in Wakayama. He had come to the United States at the age of fifteen and had built a fairly successful career as a painter, with well-reviewed exhibitions in 1925 and 1928. The two soon fell in love and began living together, although Ishigaki was married and Ayako still engaged. By this time, Ayako's fiancé Yutaka had managed to secure his family's permission to marry her. Although marriage with Yutaka would bring her economic stability and social power in Japan, while extending her stay in the United States meant living as an illegal immigrant, she decided she could not leave Eitaro or her new life. Once Eitaro obtained a divorce, Ayako enlisted the aid of her diplomat brother-in-law, who had visited New York and come away impressed by Eitaro, to obtain the reluctant consent of her father to her marriage. She and Eitaro remained together until his death in 1958.

Restless Wave glosses over somewhat the obstacles Ayako and Eitaro faced in the early part of their marriage. They had trouble making ends meet, especially after the onset of the Great Depression. Eitaro was unable to support himself as an artist or to find other work. Ayako took a number of jobs to support them, working variously as a lampshade factory worker, waitress, sales clerk, and cashier. She later stated that the intergroup and interracial camaraderie she experienced among the workers in these jobs inspired her vision of social justice.[3] In addition, Ayako took charge of housekeeping, doing tasks for which her elite upbringing had not prepared her. As she put it in a later documentary, "There were no luxuries. . . . Eitaro loved rice, which in those days was very cheap. He'd be happy with a bowl of rice and a few things sprinkled on. I'd chop up stuff to put on the rice or make my special pickles, and he'd say 'Ayako, we don't have any money but you make wonderful food,' and we'd laugh and enjoy the food."[4] During the summers, Ayako and Eitaro worked together at New York's Coney Island. Ayako sold waffles, while Eitaro staffed a skee-ball concession.

The evolution of Ayako Ishigaki's political commitment is another point of interest that is treated only briefly in *Restless Wave*, and her radical sympathies are somewhat veiled in the text. Ishigaki discusses Haru's involvement with the Farmer-Labor Party and her encounter with Korean independence groups in Japan, but remains reticent on the nature of her activities in the United States. In fact, Ayako was politically involved throughout her life in America, even though as an illegal immigrant she had no recourse if arrested and deported. Her activism was fueled by her relationship with Eitaro, a follower of the Japanese Marxist Sen Katayama. Indeed, part of what brought the two together was their shared social consciousness. In later years, Ayako frequently recounted an evening early in their relationship when Eitaro took her to Union Square, site of a mass vigil protesting the imminent execution of Sacco and Vanzetti, two Italian immigrant anarchists convicted of murder by biased courts in Massachusetts. It was this execution and the international protest it aroused, Ayako later stated, that brought home to her the dangerous potential of state power. Ayako's and Eitaro's ideas were also shaped by the Depression, which showed them the weaknesses of laissez-faire capitalism. Eitaro helped found the John Reed Club, the American Communist Party's artistic wing. In response to the Scottsboro case, the trial of a group of nine black

257

teenagers accused of raping two white women in Alabama, he completed a series of paintings of African Americans and workers. Ayako joined Eitaro in the Nihonjin Rodosha Kuabu (Japanese workers' club), a Japanese Communist organization.

In the years that followed Japan's 1931 invasion of Manchuria, Ayako took a leading role in protesting Japanese aggression in China. She felt that it was especially important for her, as a Japanese, to speak out. Her traumatic miscarriage, which is poignantly described in *Restless Wave,* also motivated her to take a stand, as the loss of her child made her reflect on the grief of mothers losing their sons in war.

Ayako became active as an organizer and speaker for left-wing antimilitarist groups such as the American Friends of the Chinese People and the American League for Peace and Democracy. To protect her family from possible reprisals by Tokyo, she adopted several pseudonyms, notably Haru Matsui. Meanwhile, she began reporting on Japan for the radical publications *The New Masses* and *China Today.* In her articles, Ayako graphically described the destructive impact of industrialism and international aggression on Japanese workers.

Ayako was particularly conscious of the connection between gender and economic exploitation. In an article on the plight of poor rural women in textile factories, she pointed out the central role of women workers in social change:

Since the invasion of Manchuria, the burden of war has weighed even more heavily on the shoulders of the masses, and the militancy of their struggles has increased. . . . In many strikes militancy and determination were shown by the girl workers, who are the most oppressed section of the working class. At the strike of the Kanto mill, 500 girls who had been locked in the dormitory escaped by climbing up over the high wall along which barbed wire had been stretched. Despite the terrorism of the gangsters hired by the company, they finally joined the other strikers at union headquarters.[5]

In 1935, Eitaro was hired by the federal Works Progress Administration to paint a mural for a new Harlem courthouse. His subject was the history of black Americans. Although he was discharged midway through the task, when the WPA restricted its hiring to American citizens, the money he earned enabled Ayako to quit her factory job and devote herself full-time to pro-Chinese activism. Soon after, Ayako was recruited by the American League for Peace and Democracy to do antifascist organizing on the West Coast.

In the spring of 1937, Ayako settled in Los Angeles, where she was hired by the Japanese American newspaper *Rafu Shimpo*. Writing under the pseudonym May Tanaka, Ishigaki began a biweekly column, "Jinsei Shokan" (women's feelings). Her writing focused on everyday life, interpolating antiwar views and feminist commentary. For example, Ishigaki praised birth control pioneer Margaret Sanger and asserted that, just as every woman was free to decide whether or not to marry, she should be free to decide whether or not to bear children.[6] Ishigaki's progressive views attracted significant positive mail, especially from women. However, when a captain in the Japanese military made a tour to encourage support for the Japanese war effort in the wake of Japan's July 1937 invasion of China, the widespread acclaim with which he was greeted by Japanese Americans made Ayako feel that she had failed, and she returned east in September.

American public opinion, fueled by media coverage of the Japanese bombing in Shanghai and reports that 100,000 people had been massacred in the capital of Nanking, was outraged by the Japanese invasion of China. The events heightened both the urgency and the popularity of Ishigaki's calls to boycott Japan. Ishigaki and Si-Lan Chen, a modern dancer and left-wing militant of Chinese and African American ancestry, made up a traveling show. The two would "debate" the Japanese invasion, and then Chen would dance. A surviving poster for Ishigaki's appearance at the Old South Church in Boston from March 1938 lists her, somewhat misleadingly, as "Miss Haru Matsui, Japanese woman, lecturer, and writer, member of the leading house of Matsui."[7] In June 1938, the *New York Times* recorded Ishigaki's passionate exhortations at a lecture in New York by the Chinese Consul-General, James Tsunechi Yu:

> Japanese planes are slaughtering thousands of Chinese civilians, and in Japan millions of people,

the people of the factories and the farms, are also suffering. They are bearing the burden of the war in high living costs, in taxation, in decreased incomes. Millions are going hungry and cold in Japan because of the war. Thousands of Japanese youths are dying in China, and not for their own cause. Japanese mothers who brought up these youths in poverty are weeping in my country as their sons, now having reached manhood, are being sent to the front to be killed. The militarists are controlling the people, suppressing their will and their desires. Japan depends on the United States for her raw materials for war. Let us boycott Japanese goods, let us prohibit the sale of war materials to Japan, and let us hope that out of this conflict there will come a more democratic form of government in my country.[8]

It was during one of Ishigaki's lectures that she was approached by a representative of Modern Age Books, a small but well-regarded progressive publisher, and invited to write a book. Ishigaki later stated that she had been troubled by the press reports of Japanese barbarism in Asia and by the Americans who asked her how the Japanese could be so cruel. She knew that her American readers would not get the point if she described the Japanese people as being as good as any other. She later wrote, "I wanted to write that the Japanese were not cruel; that they had something delicate and good, but it was militarism that distorted them. In support of this idea, I wrote about my life in Japan, and my experiences in America."[9]

CONTEMPORARY RECEPTION OF *RESTLESS WAVE*

Restless Wave appeared in late January 1940. Its style and narrative were widely praised by critics. *Saturday Review* called the book "[a]n extraordinary and very moving document"[10] while *The Nation* lauded its broad approach: "It does not purport to be a sociological treatise or an exhaustive history of the feminist movement in Japan. In lyrical, poetic terms it tells the story of a single individual who lived at a turning-point of history and of her response to new social forces."[11] Some critics adopted an orientalist discourse in discussing the atmospheric, discontinuous style of the narrative. For example, *The New Yorker* extolled the "[q]uaintly intuitive writing," and Bradford Smith commented, "There is a rich and yet womanly warp of imagery which binds the book together—a sensitiveness to landscapes, people, and inner moods which reminds one of the short imagiac poems that are Japan's best contribution to the world's poetry."[12] Some reviews responded warmly to the author's feminist message and her fundamental connection of her own struggle for independence as a woman with the cause of other oppressed groups. *New Republic*'s reviewer noted that for Ishigaki, the "emancipation [of] women, [and their] right to 'own choice' love was seen as a part of a larger struggle against a composite of social injustices."[13] Pearl S. Buck identified herself with the author: "Matsui is that most solitary of human

262

beings, a woman who cannot conform to the patterns her people have set for a woman, and the story in her book is the story of one who never found a real place for herself because she could not retire into the pattern."[14]

Ishigaki's powerful attack on Japanese society and militarism in *Restless Wave* outraged Japanese government officials, who had sporadically harassed her during the preceding years. An official from the Japanese consulate summoned Ayako and Eitaro in hopes of bribing them to do a prowar book, and threatened to get them deported if they did not agree. Although Ayako knew that her status as an illegal immigrant made her vulnerable, she refused to collaborate with Japan. The book also caused a breach between Ayako and her sister and brother-in-law. Ayako grew concerned for her family's safety after her brother-in-law, by then Japanese consul-general in San Francisco, incautiously revealed their connection to her. His recall to Japan in late 1940 eased her worries but also severed her once close ties to her sister.

Despite these sorrows, the critical and popular acclaim *Restless Wave* received greatly increased Ishigaki's fame and visibility. One effect was to seal a close friendship between Ayako and Pearl S. Buck. Ishigaki had admired Buck's *The Good Earth* for its positive portrayal of the Chinese, and she was especially touched by Buck's praise for *Restless Wave* in *Asia* magazine. She went to see Buck, who invited her to contribute to *Asia*. In September 1940, Ishigaki reviewed for the magazine Sumie Seo Mishima's *My Narrow Isle,* another book about the stultifying conditions in which Japanese women lived. She used the occasion to restate the thesis she had expounded in *Restless Wave:*

> The plight of the Japanese people today under militarism is little known to the western world. This book reveals their plight and shows that, when Japan was at peace, women were not so downtrodden. The story of Sumie Seo Mishima is the heart-rending cry of all Japanese women who try to free themselves from the yoke of feudal tradition, the struggle increased by the bitter resentment against "modernized" educated women of independence. As a Japanese woman, I know from bitter experience what she went though. It is deeply encouraging to find that the struggle of my people continues.[15]

A more practical result of *Restless Wave*'s success was that Ishigaki was able to sign with the prestigious Colston Liebow lecture bureau, which arranged appearances and press conferences for her and organized a profitable lecture tour for her with Chinese writer Helen Kuo. These lectures assured Ishigaki both a regular income and frequent public exposure. A poster from February 1941 advertises Haru Matsui's lecture on Japan as part of a series on Asia at the Fraternal Club in New York.

THE WAR YEARS—"ENEMY ALIENS"

Ishigaki was on her way to a lecture with Helen Kuo in Pittsfield, Massachusetts, on December 7, 1941, when she received word of Japan's attack on Pearl Harbor. The news stunned and saddened her. Although frightened of hostile reactions, she made her appearance that evening with the aid of a police escort and delivered her speech to a supportive crowd. In the months that followed the outbreak of war between the United States and Japan, people of Japanese ancestry throughout the country were victimized by hostility and discrimination. During 1942, over 110,000 West Coast Japanese Americans, the vast majority of whom were U.S. citizens, were summarily removed from their homes by the Army and confined in American-style concentration camps, in most cases for the balance of the war.[16] Although as East Coast residents the Ishigakis remained free from internment or mob violence, they were forced to register as enemy aliens and were subject to curfews and random searches. As a result, they destroyed much of their correspondence and other materials. They also suffered financially, as Eitaro lost his job and Ayako's lectures were cancelled. For a time, they were forced to rely on Kuo and other friends to shop for them or help in other ways. Pearl Buck sent Ayako an unsolicited letter publicly endorsing her loyalty and offering immediate aid in case of trouble, an act of faith for which she was profoundly grateful.

Ayako's situation soon began to improve. The conflict with Japan sparked new popular interest in *Restless Wave,* and during the war years, copies were given out in schools and featured in library booklists of works on Japan. Meanwhile, in March 1942, the Japanese American artist Yasuo Kuniyoshi, a longtime friend and comrade of the Ishigakis, invited Ayako to join him in

265

making Japanese-language radio broadcasts in support of Allied victory over Japan and the restoration of Japanese democracy. As a result of Ayako's appearances and of *Restless Wave,* she was recruited to work at the Japan desk of the Office of War Information (OWI). Her job was to translate Japanese-language articles from the Japanese American press in order to check on its loyalty, and to prepare newspaper releases in support of the American war effort.[17] For example, in early 1943, she wrote an article on the patriotism of Japanese Americans, pointing to the presence of Japanese American soldiers on Bataan as proof. She also wrote antiwar material for distribution to Japanese soldiers. Using microfilm of captured Japanese magazines in China, she laid out the effects of the war on Japanese society. She lost her job when the bureau moved to Denver in March 1943. Although invited to come to Denver or Washington to work as an OWI translator, Ayako refused to leave Eitaro, who was in poor health. Instead, she took a lower-paying job with the War Department, putting together a Japanese-English military dictionary in preparation for an eventual Allied invasion of Japan and writing Japanese-language articles.

Ayako continued her writing and political activities during the war. In July 1944, she lectured at Harvard University on the culture and life of Japan. She attended meetings of the Japanese American Committee for Democracy (JACD), an antifascist group in New York, and officially endorsed the JACD's Rally for Victory in the Far East in December 1944.[18] During this same period Ishigaki started a book about the wartime experience of Japanese Americans, especially soldiers.[19] She evidently worked on this book for several years, but it was never published and may never have been finished. In summer 1945, Ayako and Eitaro stayed at Yaddo, the artists' and writers' colony near Saratoga Springs, New York, where the administrators of the colony thoughtfully provided a press release to the local newspaper: "Mr. and Mrs. Ishigaki are loyal Japanese now in the employ of our government. He is in the War Department and she is in the Office of War Information."[20] While at Yaddo, Ayako became close to the famous radical writer, feminist, and pro-Chinese activist Agnes Smedley. Eitaro had met Smedley during the 1910s, and, although Ayako had not known it at the time, it was Smedley who had sent her the journal of the Japanese soldier in China that forms the last chapter of *Restless Wave.* Ayako and Eitaro would become close companions and supporters of Smedley for the rest of their time in the United States.

THE POSTWAR YEARS

In September 1945, following the atomic bombing of Hiroshima and Nagasaki by the United States, Japan surrendered. In the months that followed the end of World War II, Ayako seriously considered returning to Japan to help build democracy in her homeland. She also was anxious about arranging care for Eitaro's orphaned nieces. However, due to Eitaro's poor health and lack of interest in returning to a country he scarcely remembered, Ayako attempted to secure permanent residence for herself in the United States. On January 27, 1947, H.R. 1401, a bill "for the relief of Ayako Ishigaki (also known as Haru Matsui)" was introduced by Ellsworth Buck, a liberal Republican from New York City. It provided for her to receive permanent residence based on her "outstanding services to the United States government during the war against Japan." The bill died in committee, for reasons that are not clear.

During the early postwar years, Ayako continued to work for the War Department, writing articles on American society for magazines in occupied Japan. After her services were terminated in August 1948, Ishigaki continued to write freelance pieces for Japanese magazines under her own name and took a job writing for the *Hokubei Shimpo*, a New York newspaper. She continued her public speaking as well. In addition, at the suggestion of Pearl Buck, in October 1946 Ayako was selected to represent Japanese women at the International Assembly of Women in New York City. In an article on the conference, the *New York Times* reported her speech:

Our greatest task today is to get rid of the pro-militaristic and Fascist elements in our society . . . with the help of the democratic countries, my people can come out of the darkness into the light. . . . A discontented, underfed, under-nourished population can easily give way to prejudice, hatred, and an aggressive war—we of Japan have learned this in our past history.[21]

Similarly, in January 1947 Ishigaki spoke on the problems facing Japan at a program in Washington, D.C., sponsored by the local chapters of the East and West Association and by the Institute of Pacific Relations, and took part in a forum at the New School in New York sponsored by the National Urban League.

THE RED SCARE

By the late 1940s, America's political climate had changed drastically. *Restless Wave* went out of print and its author lost the public recognition and favor she had enjoyed. While at Yaddo in 1945, Ayako was shocked to hear the news of the atomic bomb. She later claimed that the bombing signaled the first outbreak of Cold War hysteria in the United States. During the years that followed, the wartime alliance between the United States and the Soviet Union dissolved and international tensions mounted. The Ishigakis, like many left-wing and progressive activists who had formerly worked for the government or received official endorsement, now found themselves targeted for investigation and harassment by Washington.

Government surveillance of Ayako, however, was not entirely new. Even before the end of the war, the Provost Marshal General's Office sent the Office of Strategic Services (OSS, precursor to the CIA) a report on "Haru Matsui" that described field investigations on her activities by Army Intelligence and "another agency" (presumably the FBI). The report listed several groups with which she had been involved, including the League of American

269

Writers, the American League for Peace and Democracy, and the China Aid Council, as "Communist Front" organizations. *Restless Wave* was a central text in the government's file on Ayako. While the work was found to "contain nothing of a derogatory nature" (although Modern Age Books, its publisher, was described as "Communistic in its outlook"), the government agents who drafted the report ascribed dangerous tendencies to it, using some rather inventive literary criticism:

> The theme of the book, "Restless Wave," is an indication of the character of the Subject, since the book is an autobiography. In it the heroine rebels against her father and against Japanese customs. She then marries a husband to whom her father is violently opposed. They both turned to Communism because it offers them an opportunity to fight militarism in Japan.[22]

As anticommunist hysteria mounted, Ayako felt increasingly vulnerable because of her illegal residence in the United States, although she was never issued a deportation order. She later asserted that her friendship with Agnes Smedley led to regular harassment by the FBI. When Smedley left the U.S. in 1950, she begged Ishigaki not to see her off at the dock because of the presence of FBI agents.[23] In 1951, Ayako and Eitaro, dismayed at the political climate and wishing to be reunited with their Japanese family, applied to

270

return to Japan. Before the U.S. occupation authorities could act on the request, Eitaro was arrested by the government and expelled. Ayako accompanied him back to Japan.

RETURN TO JAPAN

The Ishigakis returned to their native land in June 1951, shortly before the end of the American occupation of Japan. Eitaro suffered poor health in the years that followed, and did not exhibit his art or paint much. Instead, he devoted himself to helping Ayako make a career for herself by critiquing her writing and finding source material for her.

To earn money needed to support them both, Ayako secured work as a lecturer, journalist, and book writer. While *Restless Wave* and Ayako's prewar political activism were virtually unknown in Japan, she soon became celebrated as an authority on the United States. Ishigaki's longtime personal experience of American life was a rare and precious commodity in postwar Japan, when Japanese immigration to America was banned and money for any kind of travel was scarce. Furthermore, under the occupation, criticism of the occupying power and its policies was muted, so most Japanese received only a sugar-coated view of the United States. In this atmosphere, Ishigaki attracted widespread attention through her trenchant critiques of American society, particularly her denunciations of American racism and her analyses of McCarthyism and the American government's reactionary policy toward China.

271

In addition to her articles and lectures on American society, Ishigaki made money by bringing out translations of American books. In 1953, she published *Otoko towa onna towa*, an anthology of writings by Pearl S. Buck on a "philosophy of life for young women."[24] She also was featured as a radio commentator for NHK, although she later stated that her anti-American political views led to the cancellation of her contract.

THE "HOUSEWIFE DEBATE" AND ISHIGAKI'S FEMINISM

In the years following her return to Japan, Ishigaki became particularly notable for her feminist ideas. With the same spirit that had characterized the youthful revolt she related in *Restless Wave,* Ishigaki rebelled both in her life and her writings against the limited roles available to women in postwar Japanese society. In a number of articles, she called on Japanese women to throw off deference and passivity and struggle for independence. Her most outstanding (and notorious) effort in this regard was an article entitled "Shufu to iu dai-in shokugyō-ron" (Housewife: The second profession) that she published in the women's magazine *Fujyin Koron* in 1955. In the article, Ishigaki stridently decried the indolent and dependent existence of Japanese housewives, and snapped, "their brains have all turned to mush." While housework in Japan used to require sustained and arduous labor, Ishigaki claimed, the introduction of modern conveniences had rendered it easy and rapid, but rather than profit from their leisure by developing themselves, housewives remained starved of intellectual stimulation and increasingly infantile. Therefore, she called on Japanese women to seek outside employment, as American housewives had done. Although she acknowledged the existence of discrimination against women workers, she advised her "fellow housewives" that only amid the stimulating discipline and competition of workplace life could they achieve maturity and well-being.[25]

The article ignited a firestorm of attention, setting off the so-called "housewife debate," a set of polemics on the condition of women that dominated Japanese media for several months. Ishigaki later claimed that she was not blaming housewives for their condition or urging them to take paid labor. Rather, she explained, her point was that in the conservative atmosphere of postwar Japan, when women were finding it increasingly difficult to find jobs and were being pushed back into the home, it was only by working, even at volunteer or unpaid work, that they could find fulfillment.[26]

LATER YEARS AND LEGACY

Throughout her later years, Ayako Ishigaki continued to write prolifically, and by the time of her death she had published some thirty books and dozens of magazine articles. Her writing was notable for its colloquial and accessible style, which formed a marked contrast with the elevated language common in journalism and scholarly literature. She also was a popular television commentator, particularly as a guest on Asahi Television's

273

"Tetsuko No Heya" (one-woman interview) show. In these appearances, she struck a somewhat motherly figure, advising women on domestic topics such as aging or marital relations. She toned down considerably her feminist stance in these commentaries although she did insist that women seek equality and respect within their marriages.

Ishigaki's personal life was less than happy after Eitaro's death in 1958. In 1966, she married another Japanese artist, one whom she had known for many years, but the marriage was unsuccessful. Throughout her long widowhood she remained devoted to Eitaro's memory. Within a year of his passing, she organized a memorial exhibition and published a catalogue. In the years that followed, she wrote a biography and several articles on him and campaigned for recognition of his art. Ayako spent the last twenty years of her life purchasing Eitaro's works and raising funds to build a museum of his works in Wakayama, which opened in the 1990s. She also remained loyal to the memory of Agnes Smedley. She wrote a memoir of Smedley, *Kaiso no Sumedore,* and oversaw the posthumous publication in Japanese of Smedley's book, *Long Old Road.*

By the mid-1970s, Ishigaki's postwar writings were generally out-of-print, and she was known primarily as a women's advisor. In the years that followed, however, Japanese scholars and feminists such as Reiko Fujieda began to rediscover her and claimed her as a pioneer and an inspiration. In 1980, Horuko Sakurai did a series of serialized interviews with Ayako about her life experiences which were published in *Fujyin Koron.* In 1987, the series was published in book form.[27] Its success led to the publication three years later, on the fiftieth anniversary of its original publication, of the first-ever Japanese edition of *Restless Wave*. A biography followed in 1995. The same year, Ishigaki's diaries from the 1940s were published. Ishigaki lived her last years in a senior citizen's home, where she died in 1996.

RESTLESS WAVE AS LITERATURE AND HISTORY

Restless Wave deserves to be considered not simply as a record of the early life of one extraordinary woman, but as a wide-ranging work of history and literature. It stands as a significant early cultural studies text for our understanding of transnationalism in the American context. Ishigaki's work anticipates and resonates with many of the central questions of current-day transnationalism: Who is American, and what factors "make" an America? Is it possible to be simultaneously Asian and American? Ishigaki's narrative is—strikingly so, for her time—at once Japanese, American, and Japanese American. Unlike the African American, born with the veil, wrestling with the double consciousness in W. E. B. DuBois's narration,[28] Ishigaki acquires her veil of double consciousness—or multiple consciousness—through her crossing borders, cultures, and nations. Her narrative reveals the maturing of Haru's independent womanhood as she moves between her worlds and draws connections among them.

In the course of developing her theme of two-worldliness, the author puts in painful contrast Haru's national identity and her transnational humanitarianism and activism. Haru's identity/subjectivity is formed through the confluence of her twin struggles to liberate herself as a woman from patriarchal Japanese society and to resist the encroachment of similarly regressive attitudes in the form of class snobbery and militarism. Ishigaki continually insisted that Japanese aggression in China was not only brutal in its impact on the Chinese, but also a theft of the lives of Japan's own young men and of resources from the country's working poor, especially women. *Restless Wave* reveals how the experience of gender impacts on struggles over national identity and social justice, as Haru finds completeness as a person by addressing cross-class and international solidarity against Japanese imperialism. A striking record of the germination of feminist consciousness within dissent, the work reveals the intricacy of transnationalism as an instrument of women's liberation and Haru's use of a transnational stance as a strategy to strike a balance in her struggles for equality in gender, race, ethnicity, and class.

As a work of literature, *Restless Wave* is compulsively readable, yet subtle. *My Life in Two Worlds,* the subtitle Ishigaki gave the work, is marvelously apt—her prose, quiet and elegant, dissects the multiple sets of worlds Haru inhabits: not merely those of Japan and the United States, but also of tradition and modernity; men's and women's experience; upper class and working class; Japanese America and white America. Perhaps more than "inhabiting" two worlds, she straddles two worlds, moves between them, and eventually makes a place for herself in them. The book is a moving testament of the restless metamorphosis of women from subjugation to feudalism to a new world of modernity—a womanhood of independence. Ishigaki's narrative of crossing borders also represents early Asian women's travel writing, and the tension between the author's real-life story and the semi-fictionalized autobiographical account in the book raises issues and adds much to the study of memoirs as a genre.

In historical terms, *Restless Wave* stands as one of the first books ever written in English by a woman of Japanese ancestry. It contrasts sharply with its few predecessors, notably Etsu Sugimoto's *A Daughter of Samurai,* Kathleen Tamagawa's *Holy Prayers in a Horse's Ear,* and Shidzué Ishimoto's *Facing Two Ways,* both in content and in the quality of the writing.[29] Meanwhile, the book offers priceless firsthand testimony that enriches historical knowledge in several areas. First, it illuminates daily life in 1920s Japan, and the repressive nature of Japanese society. In particular, Ishigaki's description of the scapegoating of Koreans after the 1923 Tokyo earthquake and her tender portrait of Haru's friend who confides her Korean ancestry provide insight into the plight of Koreans under Japanese domination. In contrast, the book reveals how Japanese gender roles, which Westerners have generally assumed to be fixed and unswervingly patriarchal, were strained during the Taisho period through the influence of modern ideas. Ishigaki, who defied her family in 1921 by matriculating at Jiyu Gakuen, a women's Christian university in Tokyo, was a bridge figure in Japanese feminism; she linked the "new women" of the 1920s and the "housewife debate" of the 1950s. *Restless Wave* describes the heady freedom many young women experienced in the early 1920s and hints at the ephemeral nature of that liberation.

The last section of the book is perhaps the most intriguing as a historical document in its rare contemporary portrait of Los Angeles's Japanese American communities—all the more unusual coming from a woman of Japanese nationality—in the last years before World War II, when they were torn apart by the government's mass "evacuation" and incarceration policy. The wartime events are heavily foreshadowed in the book, both intentionally and otherwise. On the one hand, *Restless Wave* starkly describes the racial discrimination against the Issei and their Nisei (second-generation) children that preceded and undergirded the "evacuation." The author scores the Little Tokyo communities for supporting the oppressive Japanese war machine following the Japanese invasion of China, but she is careful to note that the nationalist and promilitarist attitudes of the Japanese immigrants are a direct product of their race-based isolation—and their children's—from mainstream American society. As Ishigaki relates in *Restless Wave,* it is because of the unjust treatment of the Issei, excluded from citizenship and equal rights, that Haru is able to identify herself with them in a way she could never do with Japanese at home. In an interview printed around the time the book was published, the author expressed concern over the community, and the potential harm to the Japanese Americans in case of war between the United States and Japan:

278

My people in this country suffer too much from discrimination. Their young children born here are disowning their ancient culture. They have no opportunity to learn the good things about Japan. They are exploited and unwanted. The CIO [Congress of Industrial Organizations, the federation of trade unions] has helped changed [*sic*] this situation but there is still much to be done. The American people still have to learn that many Japanese have been born here, work here, and deserve citizenship. There must be no breach of culture and ideas between father and son. We must not be ashamed to be Japanese but proud. . . . Any ill-will toward Japan on the part of the government is taken out on my people here. It is a serious problem and we must all help solve it.[30]

On the other hand, history lends a special poignancy to *Restless Wave*'s discussion of Japanese Americans, especially in the author's depiction of women at Terminal Island returning home from the factory, and the role of unionization in ending their isolation:

Japanese women in groups, three by three and five by five, overflowed from the factory gate, kicking their white calico skirts as they trudged through the sandy dust. . . . Blue-collar American trade union buttons were attached to the collars

279

of the women's dresses. One of the women, sitting in the entrance of her house, displayed the button proudly, saying that because of it her wages had been raised.[31]

Ishigaki could not know that Terminal Island would be completely taken over by the Navy in February 1942. Its houses and factories were destroyed, and its residents forced to leave with whatever they could carry on a forty-eight-hour notice.

READING *RESTLESS WAVE* NOW

The importance of *Restless Wave* extends well beyond historical and antiquarian interest. As noted, the work speaks to a number of central issues in contemporary debates over feminism, social justice, and national identity. It is a valuable lesson for those of us engaged in current-day liberation struggles to know that these ideas existed, and were on the table, long before our arrival. For example, in her description of attending a meeting on voting rights for women in the workplace and then of riding on a streetcar and observing the exhausted and shabbily dressed working women on their evening commute home, Ishigaki skillfully dramatizes in a concrete way the interaction of gender and class discrimination.[32]

Furthermore, *Restless Wave* reveals how these experiences are shaped by the question of national identity. Haru's feminist consciousness, which germinates in her individual struggle against patriarchal attitudes and class snobbery, is awakened by the struggle to resist Japanese nationalism and militarism in China, precisely because it leads to authoritarian gender and social relations in Japan. Ishigaki thus foregrounds the role of women in building cross-class and international solidarity against militarism. Haru rejects her Japanese nationality as a source of aggression, and in the service of a higher humanity maintains the possibility of an identity not linked to nation. Ishigaki's refusal to identify herself with either country or to find belonging in a national context puts *Restless Wave* in conversation with current discourse on globalization and transnationalism.

In her essay on the legacy and future of women's studies work, Inez Martinez calls for a humanitarian approach to women's studies, together with a rethinking of the concept of humanity. Martinez's forceful vision of women's studies is a fitting description of the political visions of Ayako Ishigaki:

> To begin to nudge this human history in the direction we want, we must, I believe, commit to a premise of the interconnectedness of separate beings—human to human, human to other creatures, human to the planet. . . . I implore us to resuscitate the idea of humanity and to take control of the definition of the humanities. . . . It is on the ground that we are all equally of the stuff of the universe and equally dependent on this earth that I can claim that we share basic rights.[33]

Restless Wave clearly charts the path of humanitarianism. It is exactly in that spirit that Ishigaki's Haru is able to cross many boundaries and stand strong and firm behind her vision, unwavering in spite of the most painful personal sufferings—lecturing and boycotting Japanese goods within the U.S., being barred from returning to her home country, and being denounced by her father. In many ways, her personal sufferings can be likened to those of an orphan. Her creator's positioning of her(self) as a cross-cultural female subject in transition allows her to move in and out of communities; hence, her book has an immense scope that goes far beyond the mere dramatization of her first thirty-odd years of life. In a way, we may consider *Restless Wave* as situated on the borders of many fronts: the book unfolds the bleakest moment of world history, inter-Asian politics, women's movements, labor struggles, and interethnic tension, both in Asia and the United States. As a result, what is presented to us in *Restless Wave* is the best of that legacy identified by Martinez:

> We will always have to develop self-knowledge. We will have to re-imagine our personal and social relationships. We will have to seek, articulate, and use knowledge to create more just societies. We will have to persevere. Doing that work is a lifelong challenge and a legacy I, for one, am proud to pass on to the next generation.[34]

As we read this book more than six decades after its publication, in this tumultuous time of ours, Ayako

282

Ishigaki's *Restless Wave* appears more and more a bridge across ethnic and national lines. The humanitarianism she advocates is the legacy and the future of all our work.

> Yi-Chun Tricia Lin, Borough of Manhattan
> Community College, City University
> of New York
> Greg Robinson, Université du Québec à
> Montréal
> September 2003

NOTES

This afterword is dedicated to Sanae Kawaguchi Moorehead, a friend and continuing source of inspiration.

1. Ayako Ishigaki, *Waga ai no ki ni hana miteri* (Tokyo: Fujin Gahosha, 1987), 114. English translations were prepared by Michiko Aramaki, whom the authors of this afterword wish to thank for her generous assistance.

2. For biographical material on Ishigaki, see, for example, Ayako Ishigaki, *Saraba waga Amerika: Jiyu to yokuatsu no 25-nen* (Tokyo, Senseido, 1972); Ayako Ishigaki, *Umi o watatta ai no gaka: Ishigaki Eitaro no shoga* (Tokyo: Ochanomizu Shobo, 1988); and *Waga ai no ki ni hana miteri* (Tokyo: Fujin Gahosha, 1987).

3. Ayako Ishigaki, et al., *Jidai o kangaeru: Gendai bunka zeminaru un'ei iinkai hen* (Tokyo: Dojidaisha, 1981). *Jidei o kangaeru* means "to think about the time."

4. "My Life with Him," documentary, NHK Television, Japan, ca. 1990.

5. Haru Matsui, "Factory Slaves in Japan," *China Today,* July 1935: 189–190.

6. May Tanaka (aka Ayako Ishigaki), "Jinsei Shokan," *Rafu Shimpo,* 13 September 1937, 2:2. For discussion of Ishigaki's service on *Rafu Shimpo,* see Kaori Hayashi, "History of *The Rafu Shimpo:* Evolution of a Japanese-American Newspaper, 1903–1942," (master's thesis, Department of Mass Communication, California State University, Northridge, 1990), 275–280.

7. Exhibition poster, Old South Church Archives, Boston, Massachusetts.

8. "Chinese Official Assails U.S. Policy," *New York Times,* 9 June 1938, 14:3.

9. Ishigaki, *Waga ai no ki ni hana miteri,* 115.

10. Harold Henderson, "Japan from Inside," review of *Restless*

Wave, by Haru Matsui, *Saturday Review,* 27 January 1940.

11. Elizabeth McCausland, review of *Restless Wave,* by Haru Matsui, *The Nation,* 11 May 1940.

12. Bradford Smith, review of *Restless Wave,* by Haru Matsui, *Books,* 31 March 1940.

13. Isador Schneider, "Both Sides of the China Sea," review of *Restless Wave,* by Haru Matsui, *The New Republic,* 16 September 1940.

14. Pearl S. Buck, review of *Restless Wave,* by Haru Matsui, *Asia,* March 1940: 165.

15. Haru Matsui, "Bookshelf," *Asia,* September 1940.

16. For more information about the internment of Japanese Americans, see, for example, Greg Robinson, *By Order of the President: FDR and the Internment of Japanese Americans* (Cambridge: Harvard UP, 2001).

17. Materials on Ishigaki's writings for OWI are not collected, although correspondence related to her activities for the agency are in the papers of the director, Japan Section, Foreign Language Divison, Office of War Information, Record Group 208, National Archives.

18. *JACD Newsletter,* December 1944.

19. *Pacific Citizen,* 22 July 1944.

20. Janice R. Mackinnon and Steven R. Mackinnon, *Agnes Smedley: The Life and Times of an American Radical,* (Berkeley: U of California P, 1988), 295.

21. "Argentine Woman Assails Dictators," *New York Times,* 25 October 1946, 5:1.

22. Major Clarence R. Herbert, CMP to Office of Strategic Services, 17 February 1945, Box 1731, Office of Strategic Services Files, Provost Marshal General's Office Records, RG 389, National Archives, Washington, D.C.

23. Mackinnon and Mackinnon, 337.

24. Ayako Ishigaki, *Otoko towa onna towa,* (Tokyo:

Shinhyoronsha, 1953). The book was adapted from Pearl S. Buck, *Of Men and Women* (New York: John Day Company, 1941), a work whose feminist message prefigured and clearly influenced Ishigaki's.

25. Jan Bardsley, "Discourse on Women in Postwar Japan: The Housewife Debate of 1955," *U.S.–Japan Women's Journal,* English Supplement 16 (1999): 5–7.

26. *Jidei o kangaeru,* 118.

27. Ishigaki, *Waga ai no ki ni hana miteri,* op. cit.

28. W. E. B. DuBois, *The Souls of Black Folk,* 1903.

29. See Etsu Inagaki Sugimoto, *A Daughter of Samurai* (New York: Doubleday, 1925); Kathleen Tamagawa, *Holy Prayers in a Horse's Ear* (New York, Ray Long & Richard R. Smith, 1932); Shidzué Ishimoto, *Facing Two Ways: The Story of My Life* (Stanford: Stanford UP, 1963 [1935]).

30. Louise Mitchell, "Rebellious Daughter of Japan Who Fights for China Freedom," *The Daily Worker,* 13 February 1940, 7:1.

31. Haru Matsui, *Restless Wave* (New York: Feminist Press, 2004 [1940]), 230–231.

32. For Ishigaki's writing as "proletarian sublime," see Michael Denning, *Cultural Front: The Laboring of American Culture in the Twentieth Century* (London, New York: Verso, 1996) 145–46.

33. Inez Martinez, "Legacy," *Women's Studies Quarterly* 30:3–4 (fall/winter 2002), 36.

34. Ibid., 40.

Culture. $26.95 cloth.

Miss Giardino, a novel by Dorothy Bryant. $11.95 paper, $32.00 cloth.

Mulberry and Peach: Two Women of China, a novel by Hualing Nieh. $12.95 paper.

No Sweetness Here and Other Stories, by Ama Ata Aidoo. $10.95 paper, $29.00 cloth.

Paper Fish, a novel by Tina De Rosa. $15.95 paper, $20.00 cloth.

The Present Moment, a novel by Marjorie Oludhe Macgoye. $11.95 paper, $30.00 cloth.

Proud Man, a novel by Katherine Burdekin (aka Murray Constantine). $14.95 paper, $35.00 cloth.

Reena and Other Stories, by Paule Marshall. $11.95 paper.

Shedding and Literally Dreaming, by Verena Stefan. $14.95 paper, $32.50 cloth.

The Right Thing to Do, a novel by Josephine Gattuso Hendin. $13.95 paper.

The Silent Duchess, a novel by Dacia Maraini. $14.95 paper, $19.95 hardcover.

Sister Gin, a novel by June Arnold. $12.95 paper.

Skyscraper, a novel by Faith Baldwin. $14.95 paper.

The Slate of Life: More Contemporary Stories by Women Writers of India. $12.95 paper, $35.00 cloth.

Sultana's Dream: Selections from "The Secluded Ones," by Rokeya Sakhawat Hossain. $8.95 paper, $19.95 cloth.

Swastika Night, a novel by Katharine Burdekin. $10.95 paper.

The Test, a novel by Dorothy Bryant. $13.95 paper.

The Tree and the Vine, a novel by Dola de Jong. $9.95 paper, $27.95 cloth.

Truth Tales: Contemporary Stories by Women Writers of India. $13.95 paper, $35.00 cloth.

Two Dreams: New and Selected Stories, by Shirley Geok-lin Lim. $10.95 paper, $24.00 cloth.

Umbertina, a novel by Helen Barolini. $18.95 paper.

Unpunished: A Mystery, by Charlotte Perkins Gilman. $10.95 paper, $18.95 cloth.

Unspeakable Women: Selected Short Stories Written by Italian Women During Fascism. $14.95 paper, $35.00 cloth.

Wall Tappings: An International Anthology of Women's Prison

Writings, 200 to the Present. $18.95 paper, $49.00 cloth.

Women on War: An International Anthology of Writings from Antiquity to the Present. $19.95 paper.

What Did Miss Darrington See? An Anthology of Feminist Supernatural Fiction. $14.95 paper.

Winter's Edge, a novel by Valerie Miner. $10.95 paper.

With Wings: An Anthology of Literature by and About Women with Disabilities. $14.95 paper.

Women Working: An Anthology of Stories and Poems. $13.95 paper.

Women Writing Africa: The Southern Region (Vol. 1). $29.95 paper, $75.00 cloth.

Women Writing in India, Vol. I: 600 B.C. to the Early Twentieth Century. $29.95 paper, $59.95 cloth.

Women Writing in India, Vol. II: The Twentieth Century. $32.00 paper, $59.95 cloth.

You Can't Get Lost in Cape Town, a novel by Zoë Wicomb. $13.95 paper, $42.00 cloth.

To receive a free catalog of the Feminist Press's 200 titles, call or write the Feminist Press at the City University of New York, 365 Fifth Avenue, Suite 5406, New York, NY 10016; phone: (212) 817–7920; fax: (212) 817–1593. Feminist Press books are available at bookstores or can be ordered directly at www.feministpress.org. Send check or money order (in U.S. dollars drawn on a U.S. bank) payable to the Feminist Press. Please add $4.00 shipping and handling for the first book and $1.00 for each additional book. VISA, MasterCard, and American Express are accepted for telephone and secure Internet orders. Prices subject to change.